Digitization is the need of the time. In the future, training in industrial training institutes will need to be conducted using online internet to make training more convenient and easy. E-books containing a set of MCQ questions will be made available to the trainees as they need to be more accustomed to the multiple choice questions MCQ to prepare for the online exams taking place in their industrial training institutes.

With all these factors in mind, Mr. Manoj Madhukar Dole Instructor, Industrial Training Institute, Satara, has written books according to the new annual system and NSQF-5 syllabus. And they've created theoretical mobile apps and blogs to make training easier, and made all these educational materials available for download on the world famous websites Google Play Store, Amazon and Apple Book Store.

The books were published by Hon'ble Joint Director Shri Rajendra Ghume Saheb Regional Office of Vocational Education and Training, Pune on 9/1/2019, at this time Shri Prakash Saigavkar Saheb Principal Government Industrial Training Institute Aundh Pune, Shri Tukaram Misal Saheb Principal Govt. Q. Sanstha Satara, Shri Sachin Dhumal Saheb District Vocational Education and Training Officer Satara, Shri Yatin Pargaonkar Saheb Principal Govt. Q. Sanstha Kolhapur, Shri Vikas Teke Saheb Inspector Vocational Education and Training Regional Office Pune, Palekar Foods Products Pvt. Ltd. Entrepreneurial Chairman of Satara Mr. Nilkanthrao Palekar Saheb, Chairman of Hira Foods Mr. Ibrahim Baba Tamboli Saheb, Mrs. Shalmali Pawar Headmaster Government Technical School Center Satara and other dignitaries were present on the occasion.

TOOL & DIE MAKER FIRST YEAR (PRESS TOOLS, JIGS & FIXTURES) DIES & MOULDS MCQ

OBJECTIVE QUESTION ANSWERS

MANOJ DOLE

Contents

Prologue

Tool & Die Maker First Year (Press Tools, Jigs & Fixtures) Dies & Moulds is a simple Book for ITI Engineering Course Tool & Die Maker (Press Tools, Jigs & Fixtures) Dies & Moulds , First Year, Sem- 1 & 2, Revised NSQ F-5 Syllabus in 2022, It contains objective questions with underlined & bold correct answers MCQ covering all topics including all about fitting covering components like filing, sawing, drilling, tapping, chipping, grinding and different fits, turning operations on lathe viz., plain, facing, boring, grooving, step turning, parting, chamfering, knurling and different thread cutting by setting the different parameter, Different milling operations (plain, stepped, angular, dovetail, T-slot, contour, gear) along with surface & cylindrical grinding to an accuracy of ±0.02mm, solid modeling of mould in CAD & Pro E taught setting and execution of welding and lots more.

We add new question answers with each new version. Please email us in case of any errors/omissions. This is arguably the largest and best e-Book for All engineering multiple choice questions and answers.

As a student you can use it for your exam prep. This e-Book is also useful for professors to refresh material.

Prologue

Foreword

Vocational education and training is imparted through the Department of Vocational Education and Training through the Department of Business Education and Business Practical to supply multi-skilled artisans in line with the rapidly growing demand in the industrial sector in the 21st century. All the occupations within the institutions are important, as the trainees from these occupations develop multi-skills as per the demands of the industry.

with the noble intention of making available MCQ e-books suitable for all businesses, considering that all the examinations in all the industries in the industrial sector are conducted online and include MCQ method questions. Mr. Manoj Madhukar Dole has written a very good e-book on MCQ method as per the new annual syllabus. This e-book will definitely be a guide for all the trainees, trainee candidates, training instructors and others concerned.

The author of the book is Mr. Manoj Madhukar Dole, Instructor Gov. ITI Satara has 17 years of training experience. Written as a new annual pattern, this e-book incorporates modern digital QR Code technology to understand the layout, simple language, and simple syntax, diagrams and videos for each subject. So I am sure that this e-book will definitely be useful for in-depth study and exam practice. The work they have done is certainly commendable.

Mr. Tukaram Misal
Principal Government Industrial Training Institute Satara.

Preface

DGET New Delhi and CSTARI Kolkata have been implementing an annual pattern for all businesses in ITI since the August 2018 session. The examination system will also be changed and it will be online from this year and since all the questions are of Objective Type (MCQ), the trainees are in dire need of in-depth study. It is with this in mind that we are delighted to present the books based on the old NIMI pattern and a complete overview of the new annual pattern, and we hope that these books will be a guide for all business directors and trainees. Is.

For writing these books, Johar Awate Saheb, Principal of ITI Akluj. Former Principal of ITI Satara Saigavkar Saheb, Assistant Director Shri Chandrakant Dhekne Saheb Regional Office of Vocational Education and Training, Pune, District Vocational Education and Training Officer Sachin Dhumal Saheb and Headmaster Government Technical School Kendra Shalmali Pawar Madam and son Adhiraj Dole, mother Kusum Dole, I am very grateful to my father Madhukar Dole and wife Ashwini Dole for their special guidance and cooperation from time to time.

Also, in a very short period of time, the book was reviewed by Shri Rajendra Ghume Saheb, Joint Director, Vocational Education and Training Regional Office, Pune, for his invaluable time in publishing the book. I am sincerely grateful for their feedback.

I am grateful to the Instructor of ITI Satara for there continuous support from the very beginning of writing the book.

From this book, I consider myself blessed to have shared my thoughts on e-learning with you. I will not claim that this book is perfect, because considering the perfection, this book is an attempt and is in its infancy. They will be valuable for improvement if they are tested and suggested.

Manoj Dole
Dated 9/1/2019

Preface

Acknowledgements

The industrial training and theoretical examination system of our industrial training institutes and these changes have been accepted by the craft instructors and the trainees. Theoretical examinations conducted in your industrial training institutes are also conducted online. Since these examinations are of multiple choice MCQ method, the trainees will need to get more practice of such questions.

With all these considerations in mind, Mr. Manoj Madhukar, Director, Dole Crafts, Katari Industrial Training Institute, Satara, has done a thorough study and with his diligent work and added his keen intellect, according to the new annual system and NSQF-5 syllabus, e-book of Katari and other machine trades. -Book) and they have created mobile apps and blogs on theoretical topics to make training easier and have made all these educational materials available for download on the world famous websites Google Play Store, Amazon and Apple Book Store. Training has been made easier by creating a print version and using advanced techniques like QR Code.

All these educational materials will definitely be a guide for all the trainees for in-depth study and for the craft instructors and other concerned who are imparting vocational training.

CHAPTER ONE

Tool & Die Maker First Year MCQ Drawing

Online Test Exam
ITI Books
CNC Course
AutoCAD CAM
JOB & Apprentice
Online Theory
Computer Course
Trading Course
Web Designing
MSCIT Course
Shopping Business
Internet Business
Remotasks Course
Online Services
Top Sportsmans
Indian Army
Freedom Fighters
Top Scientists
Social Reformers
Motivational Speaker
Top Richest People
Join WhatsApp Group
Join Facebook Group
Like Facebook Page
PAN / Adhar / Licence
Passport

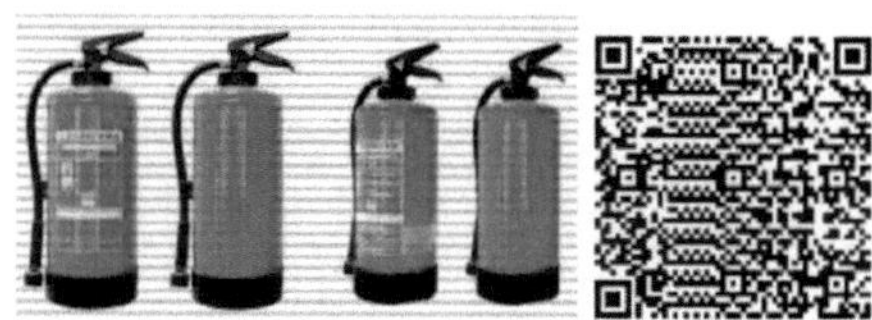

Fire extinguisher

Calliper

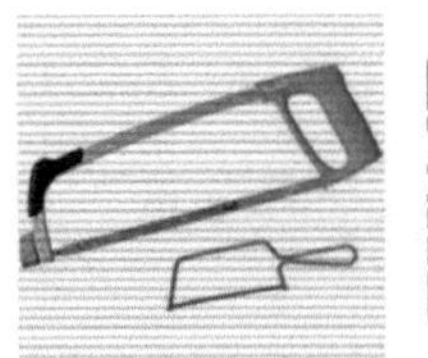 

Hacksaw frame

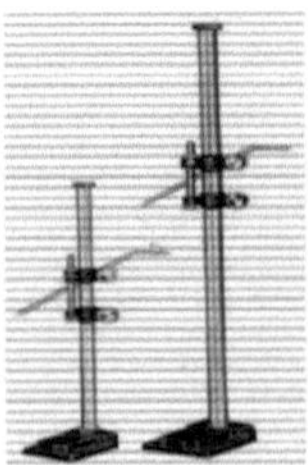 

Universal surface guage

Hammer

Centre punch

Bench vice

Files

Scraper

Surface Plate

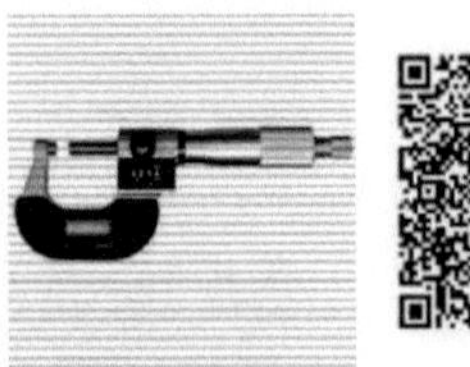

Outside Micrometer

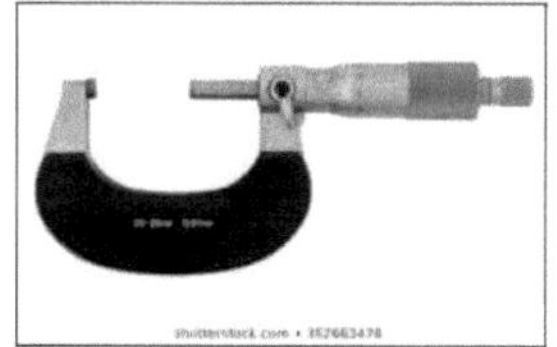

Micrometer

Depth micrometer

Vernier Calliper

Vernier bevel protractor

Drilling

Reamer

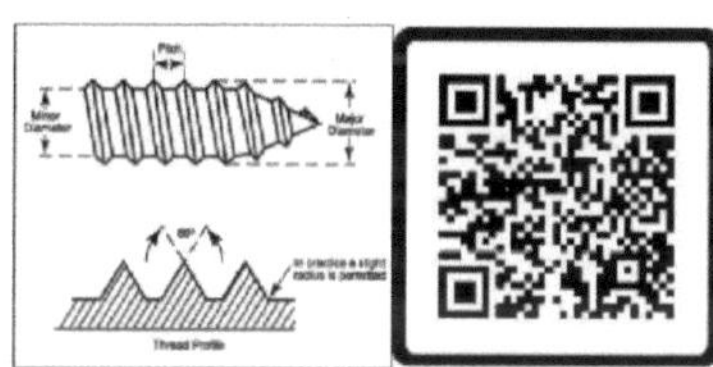

Thread

Tap Die

Grinding Wheel

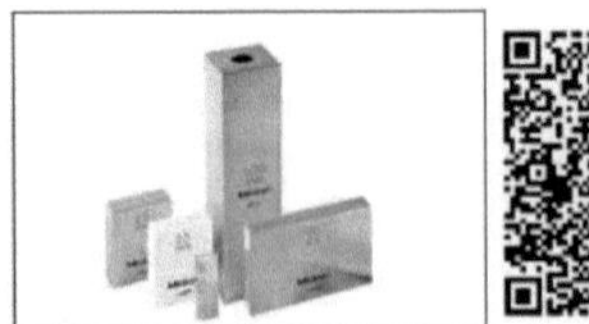

Slip gauge

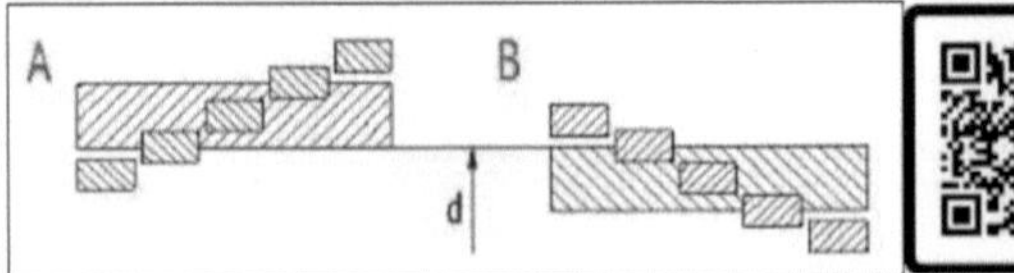

Limit fit tolerance

Lathe Machine

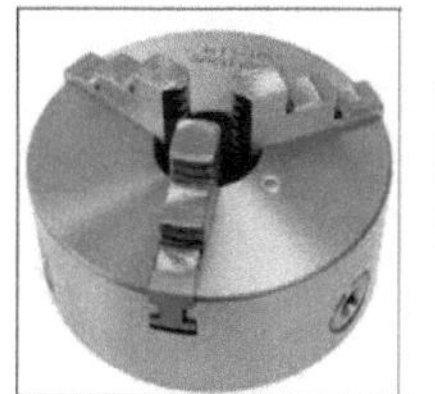

Lathe chuck

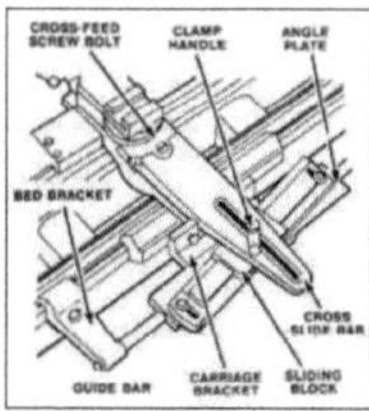

Taper turning attachment

taper ring gauge

screw pitch gauge

Gear

screw pitch gauge

Tap Die

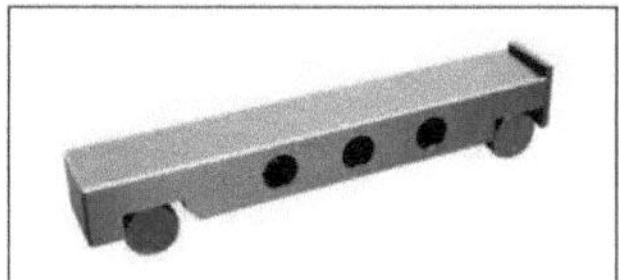 

Sine bar

Slip gauge

Dial test indicator

Telescopic gauge

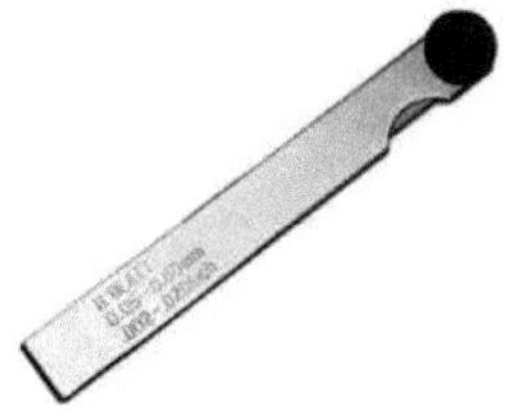

Feeler gauge

Centre gauge

Jig

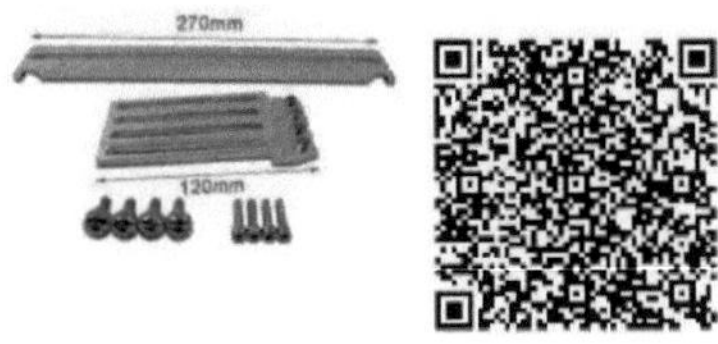

Fixture

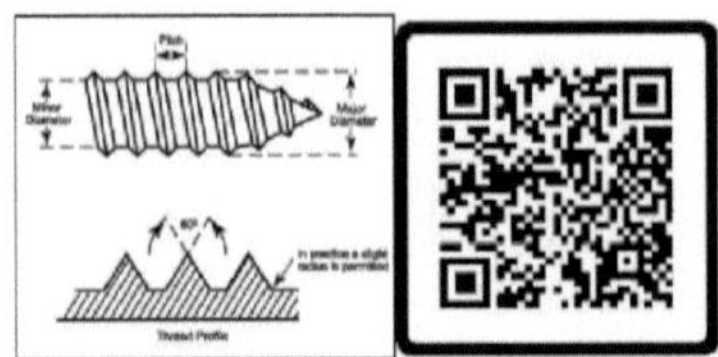

Thread

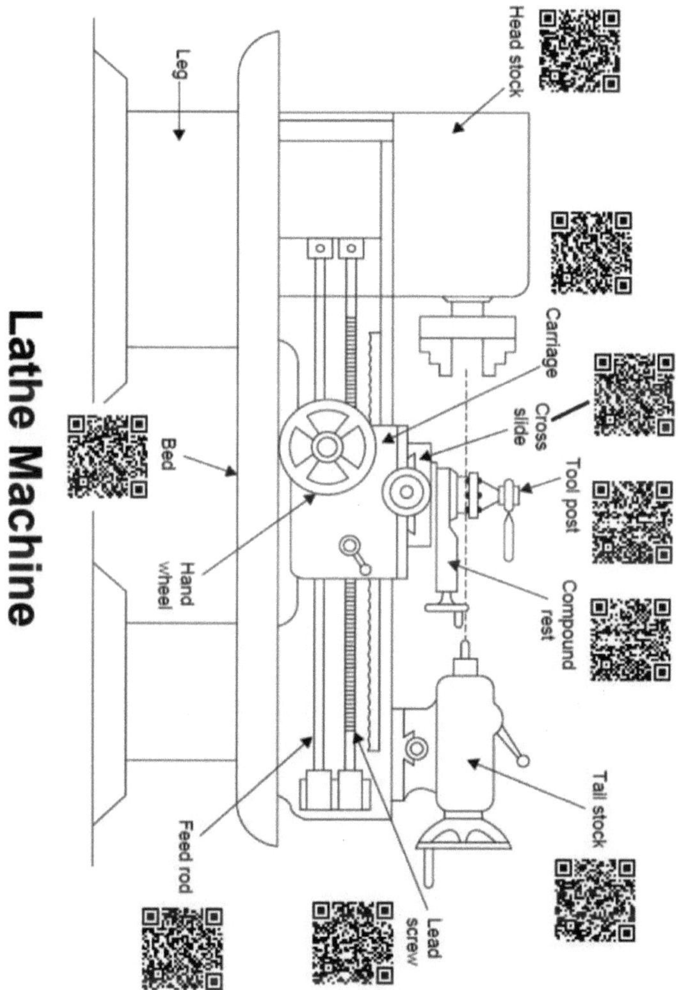
Lathe Machine
Head stock
Leg
Carriage
Cross slide
Tool post
Compound rest
Bed
Hand wheel
Tail stock
Feed rod
Lead screw

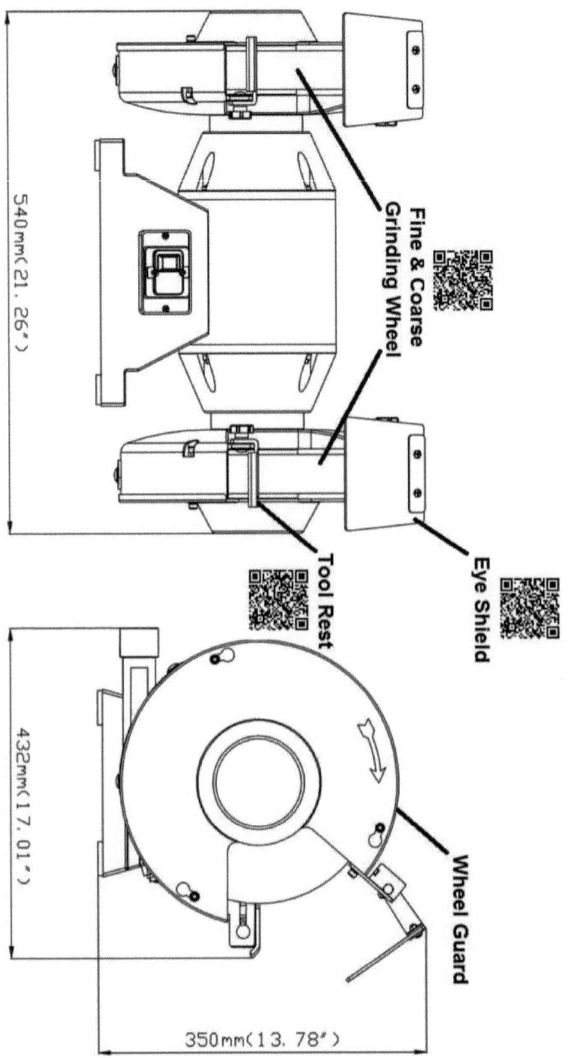
Bench Grinding Machine
Fine & Coarse Grinding Wheel
Eye Shield
Tool Rest
Wheel Guard
540mm(21.26")
432mm(17.01")
350mm(13.78")

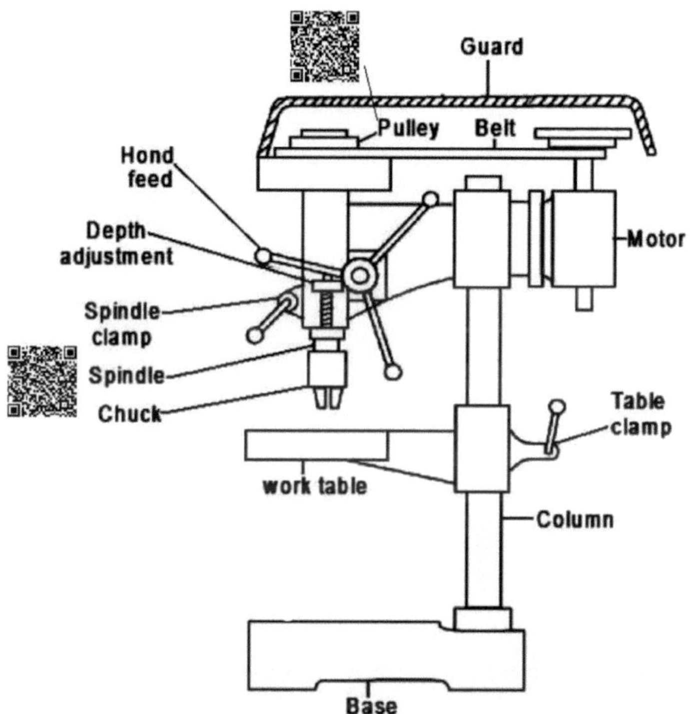

Piller Drilling Machine

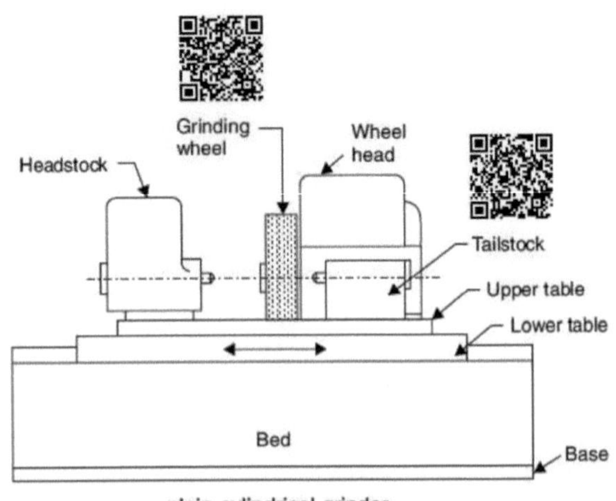

plain cylindrical grinder

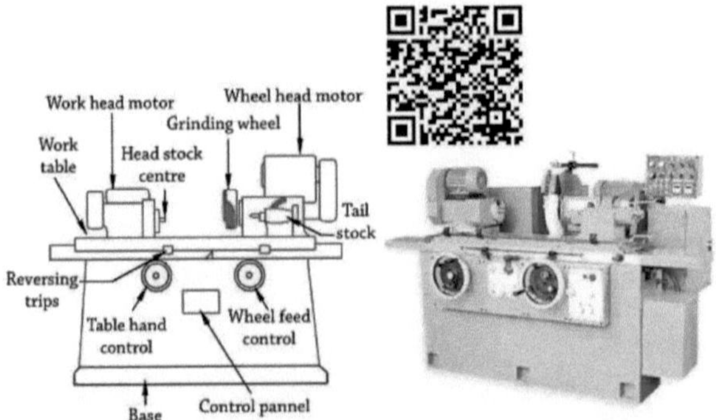

Cylindrical grinding machine

To study Different operations and parts of Surface Grinding Machine

SURFACE GRINDER

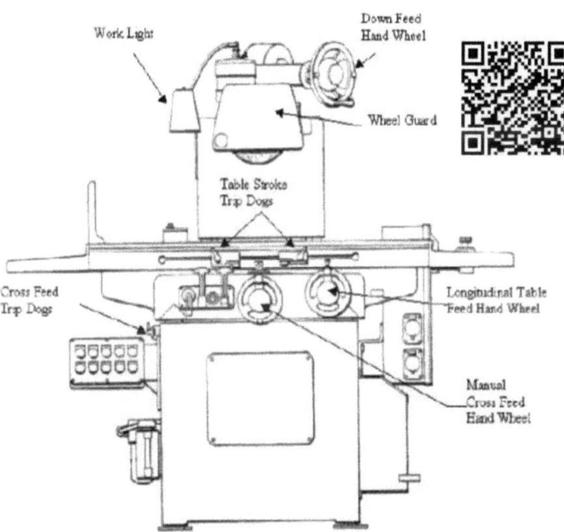

Surface grinding is used to produce a smooth finish on flat surfaces. It is a widely used abrasive machining process in which a spinning wheel covered in rough particles (grinding wheel) cuts

PLAIN OR HORIZONTAL MILLING MACHINE

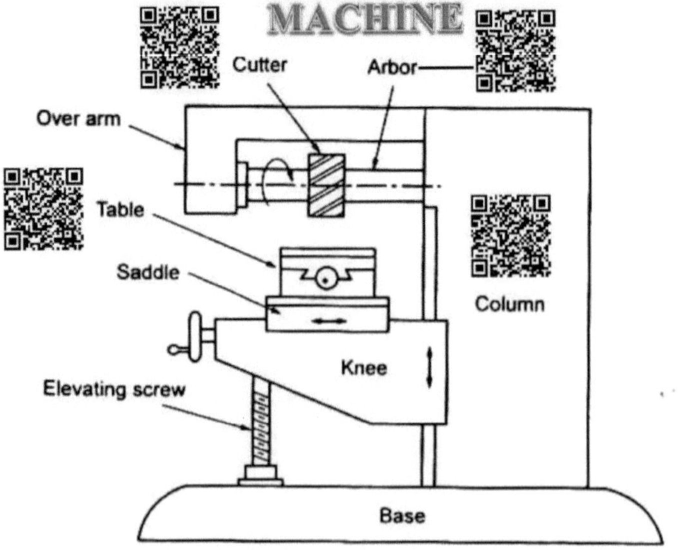

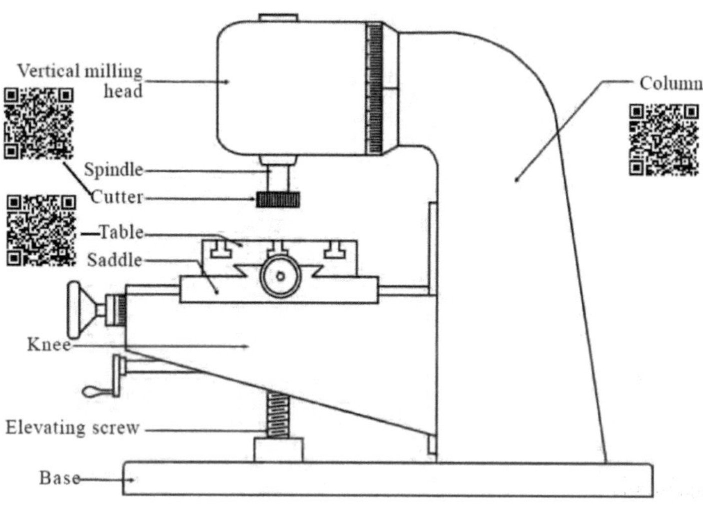

Vertical Milling Machine

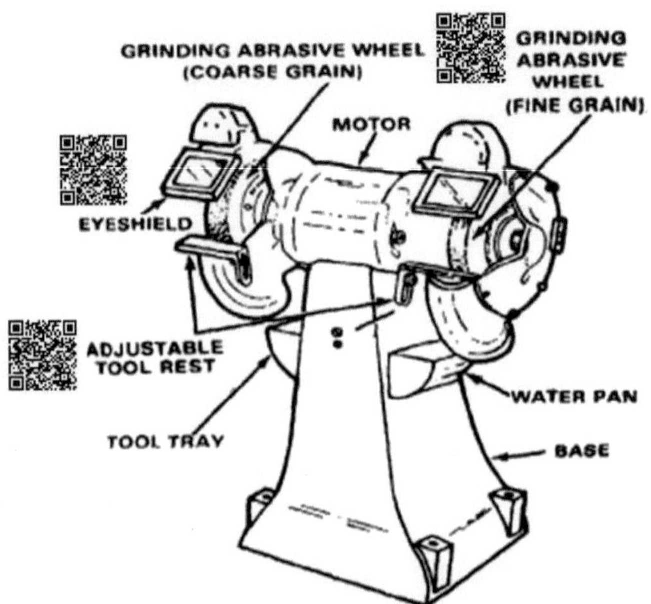

Pedastal Grinding Machine

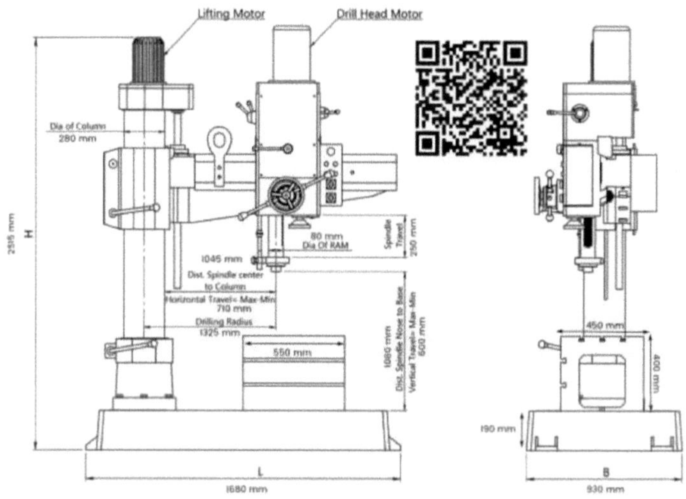

Radial Drilling Machine

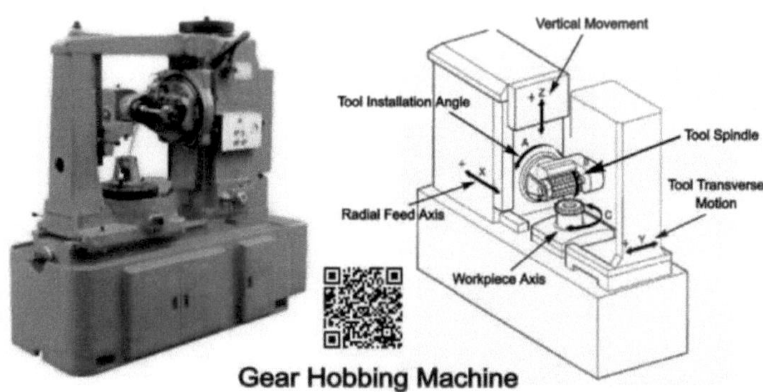

Gear Hobbing Machine

DOUBLE HOUSING PLANER

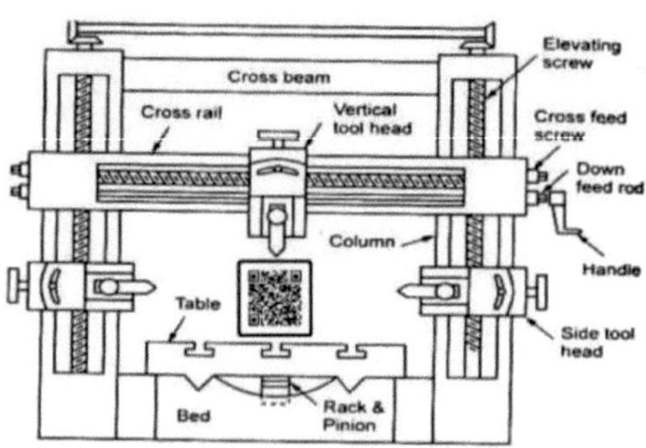

PIT PLANER

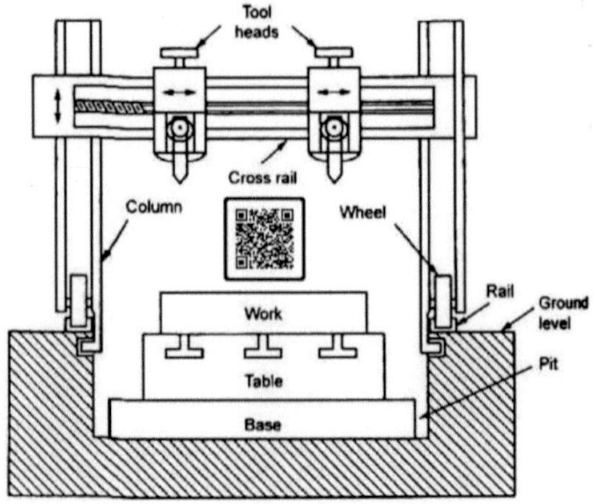

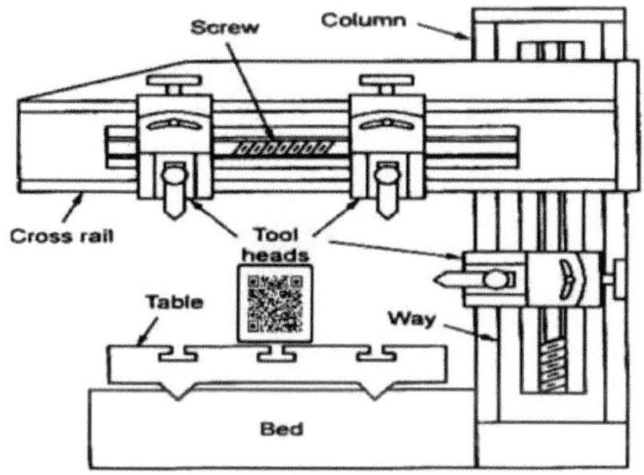

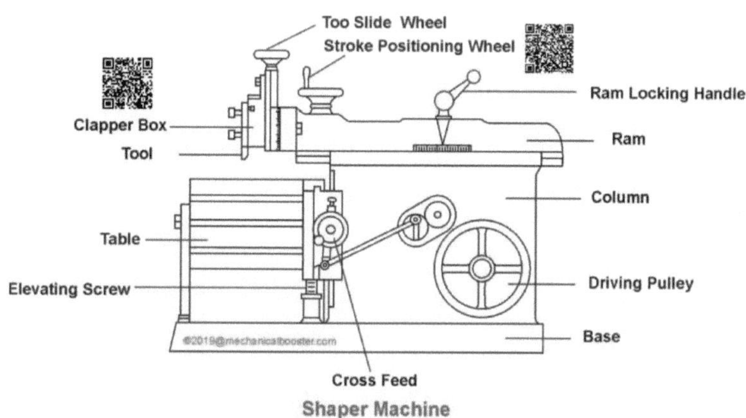

Shaper Machine

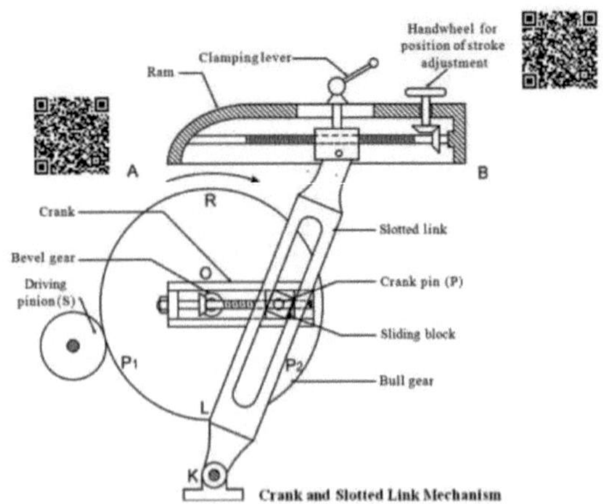

Quick Return Mechanism of Shaper Machine

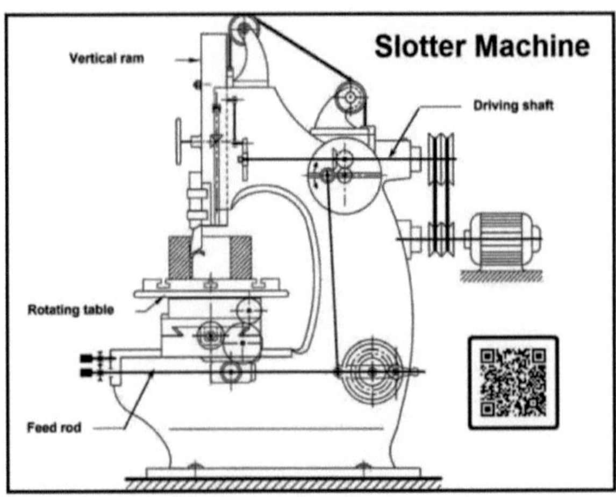

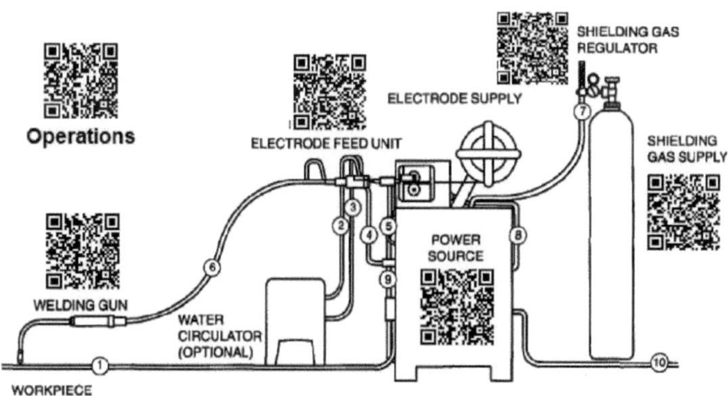

Gas Metal Arc Welding

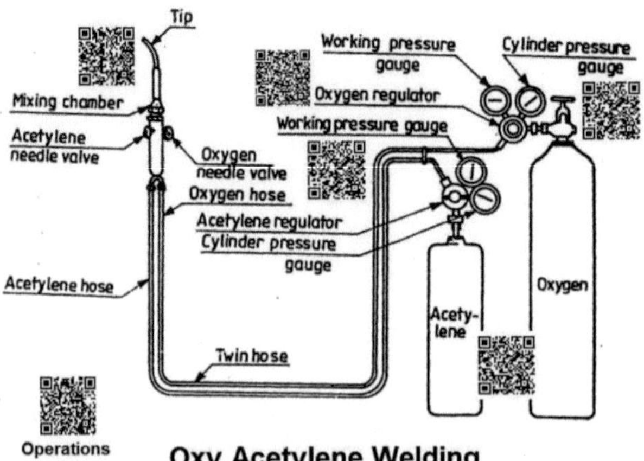

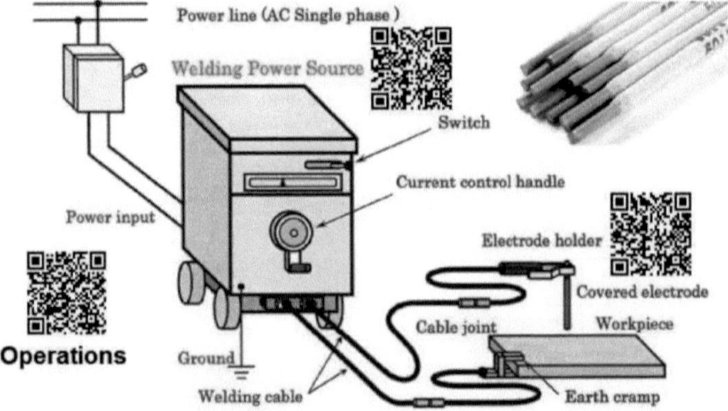

Shielded Metal Arc Welding

Enter Caption

CHAPTER TWO

Tool & Die Maker First Year MCQ

01] In case of bleeding, take treatment Of

D] cold 3" and rest

<u>A] spray cold water</u>

B] Bandage immediately -----

B] Enquire about the accident thought treatment

02] in case of an accident, the victim should im

A] Asked to take rest

<u>C] Attended immediately</u>

D] leave him

03] First aid is given to an injured or ill person primarily

A] Save life

B] Prevent further deterioration of the muff's

C] Give best possible comfort

<u>D] All of these</u>

04] Colour code for Bins for waste paper segregation is -----

<u>A] blue Colour</u>

B] Yellow Colour

C] Red Colour

D] Green Colour

05] In Japanese Seiko stands for -------------

<u>A] Shine</u>

B] Sort

C] Standardize

D] Sustain

06] Benefit of SS system is ------

A] Increase in productivity

B] Increase in quality

C] Reduction in wastage of time

D] All of these

07] Safety is -----------

A] nobody's business

B] every bodise business

C] Some bodies business

D] The organization business

08] For basic categories of safety signs are available The meaning of"prohibition" sign ----

A] shows it must not be done

B] Shows what must be done

C] Warns the hazard or danger

D] Gives information of safety provision

09] Which one is a workshop safety?

A] Keep shop floor clean and free from grease, oil or other slippery materials

B] Stop the machine before changing the speed

C] Don't use cracked or chipped tools

D] Don't try to stop a running machine with hand

10] In Personal Protect Equipment (PPE] HELMET is used to

A] protect head

B] Protect eyes

C] Protect hands

D] Protect ears

11] Which of the following belongs to general safety?

A Have a worker in good attitude

B] The work clean and clear

C] Concentrate on your work

D] Keep the floor and gangways clean and clear

12] While grinding, which is used to protect the eyes?

A] Dark green glass

B] Mask

C] Sun glasses

D] Safety goggles

13] Which of the following is done for machine safety?

A] Check the oil level before starting the machine

B] Do things in a methodical way

C] Keep the floor and gangways clean and clear

D] Don't use dies and scarves

14] In Personal Protect Equipment (PPE], 'sleeves' is used to protect ----------

A] Face

B] Eyes

C] Ears

D] Hands

15] ABC stands for --------------

A] Automatic Breathing Control

B] Automatic Blood Control

C] Airway Breathing Circulation

D] Automatic Blood Circulation

04] Fire & FIRE EXTINGUISHERS

fire extinguisher

16] To put off"Class B" fire, the types of fire extinguisher used is

A] dry power

B] Carbon dioxide

C] Jet of water

D] Foam type

17] Which type of fire extinguisher is used to put off general fire?

A] Water type Extinguisher

B] Foam type Extinguisher

C] Dry chemical powder Extinguisher

D] Carbon dioxide (C02] Extinguisher

18] One micrometer (U] is equal to

A] 01mm

B] 001mm

C] 0001mm

D] 00001mm

19] The caliper meant for measuring the width of a slot is

A] Odd leg caliper

B] Outside caliper

C] Jenny caliper

D] Inside calliper

Callipers

20] The size of the dividers are specified by the -----------

A] Total length of legs

B] Distance between the points when fully opened

C] Length of legs without points

D] distance between the pivot and the point

21] The instrument used to mark parallel lines, parallel to the datum edge is -

A] jenny caliper

B] Divider

C] Outside calliper

D] Inside calliper

22] Which one of the following is an indirect measuring tool?

A] Outside caliper

B] Vernier calliper

C] Steel rule

D] Outside micrometer

23] For cutting thin tubing, the most suitable pitch of the hacksaw blade is

A] 18mm

B] 14mm

C] 1mm

D] 08mm

Hacksaw frame

24] For cutting solid brass, the most suitable pitch of the hacksaw blade is

A] 18mm

B] 14mm

C] 1mm

D] 08mm

25] A new hacksaw blade after a few strokes becomes loose because of the

A] Stretching of the blade

B] Wing-nut threads being worn out

C] Wrong pitch of the blade

D] Improper selection of the set of saws

26] While cutting small diameter pipes, it is advisable to watch regularly and ensure that

A] The cut is along the curved line

B] More saw teeth are in contract

C] The work is not overheated

D] Proper balancing of hacksaw is maintained

27] The vice clamps are used to

A] Protect hard jaws

B] Clamp the work pieces rigidly

C] Protect the finished surfaces

D] Prevent the movable jaw being filed

28] The reference surface during marking is provided by the

A] Surface gauge

B] Workpiece

C] Drawing of the work

D] Marking table surface

29] The size of an engineer's vice is specified by the

A] Length of the movable jaw

B] Width of the jaws

C] Height of the vice

D] Maximum opening of the jaws

30] The part of the universal surface gauge which helps to draw a parallel line along a datum edge is the

A] Rocker arm

B] Snug

C] Fine adjustment screw

D] Guide pins

31] Scribers are made of

A] Mild steel

B] High carbon steel

C] Brass

D] Cast iron

32] Portion of the hammer used for fixing the handle is

A] Face

B] Peen

C] Cheek

D] Eye hole

Hammer

33] Weight of the hammer for the marking purpose is

A] 250g

B] 500g

C] 1 kg

D] 2 kgs

34] The size of the dividers are specified by the

A] Total length of the legs

B] Distance between the points when fully opened

C] Length of legs without the points

D] Distance between the pivot and the point

35] The included angle of the groove of 'V' block is always

A] 45°

B] 60°

C] 90°

D] 120°

36] 'V' blocks are available in grades of

A] A & B

B] A,B & C

C] 1,2 & 3

D] 1 & 2

37] 'V' blocks of grade 'B' are made of

A] Cast iron

B] Mild steel

C] Steel

D] Cast steel

38] Name the punch used to locate the centre

A] Prick punch 30°

B] Prick punch 60°

C] Centre punch

D] Dot punch

centre punch

39] The point angle of centre punch is --------

A] 30°

B] 50°

c] 900

D] 1200

40] Punches are used for forming ---------of any shape

A] Holes

B] Mining

C] Knurling

D] Reaming

41] Generally the length of the handle of the vice is ----------

A] 15 times the normal size of the vice

B] 25 times the normal size of the vice

C] 35 times the normal size of the vice

D] 45 times the normal size of the vice

Bench vice

42] Bench vice spindle is made of
A] mild steel
B] Cast iron
C] Tool steel
D] Bronze
43] The convexity of files helps
A] To file concave surfaces
B] To file convex surfaces
C] To prevent rounding of edges of work
D] The file to become straight when pressure is applied
44] Which file used for filling wood, leather and other soft material?
A] Single cut file
B] Double cut file
c] Rasp cut file
D] Curved cut file
45] File used is used for ------------
A] Cleaning the work piece
C] Renewing the file teeth
B] cleaning the file teeth
D] Cleaning the chips
46] File card is used to --------
A] Clean the work piece
C] Renew the file teeth
B] Clean the file teeth
47] The point angle of scriber is -----------
A] 30°
B] 60°
C] 5° to 10°
D] 12° to 15°
48] The cutting angle for chipping cast iron is
A] 375°
B] 55°
C] 60°
D] 90°
49] The chisel will dig into the material when
A] The rake angle is more
B] The clearance angle is too low
C] The angle of inclination is more

D] The angle of inclination is too low

50] A slight convexity is given to the cutting edge to

A] Cut curved surfaces

B] Cut sharp corners

C] Prevent digging of the ends

D] Allow the lubricant to enter

51] Surface plates are made of

A] High grade cast steel

B] Fine-grained cast iron

C] Alloy steels

D] Wrought iron

52] The least count of vernier calliper is (main scale = 49 division, vernier scale = 50 division]

A] 0.1 mm

B] 0.01 mm

C] 0.001 mm

D] 0.02 mm

53] The type of measurement made by using a Vernier Calliper is -------

A] Direct measurement

B] Indirect measurement

C] 90“] (a] 81 (b]

D] None of these

54] Accuracy or least count of a metric outside micrometer is ---------

A] 0-1 mm

B] 0.01 mm

C] 0.001 mm

D] 0.02 mm

55] 1000 microns means -----

A] 1 mm

B] 1 m

C] 1000 mm

D] 10 cm

56] in a metric micrometer, a complete revolution of thimble advances -----------

A] 0.01 mm

B] 0.25 mm

C] 0.50 mm

D] 100mm

57] Ratchet Stop in the micrometer helps to ------------

A] Control the pressure

B] lock the spindle

C] Adjust the zero error

D] Hold the work piece

58] 1000 micron means ------------

A] 1 mm

B] 1 m

C] 1000 mm

D] 10 cm

59] What is the zero reading of a 50-75 mm outside micrometer?

A] 0000 mm

B] 001 mm

C] 2500 mm

D] 5000 mm

Micrometer

60] The value of the smallest division on sleeve of a metric outside micrometer is -----

A] 050 mm

B] 100 mm

C] 150 mm

D] 200 mm

61] Ratchet stop in the micrometer helps to ---------

A] control the pressure

B] Lock the spindle

C] Adjust the zero error

D] Hold the work piece

62] The least count of a vernier height gauge in the metric system is

A] 0.05 mm

B] 0.1 mm

C] 0.02 mm

D] 0.001 mm

63] The least count of a vernier height gauge in the british system is

A] 0.05”

B] 0.001”

C] 0.002”

D] 1”

Vernier height gauge

64] For marking purposes, a vernier height gauge must be used on the

A] bed of a machine tool

B] surface plate

C] square block

D] any flat surface

65] The reading of a vernier height gauge is similar to that of a

A] vernier caliper

B] depth micrometer

C] dial test indicator

D] gauge

66] The part which slides on the beam of a vernier height gauge is known as a

A] base

B] beam scale

C] scriber

D] vernier slide

67] The size of a vernier height gauge is specified by the

A] height of the vernier scale

B] height of the beam

C] width of the beam

D] size of the base

68] The base of the vernier height gauge is generally made out of

A] cast iron

B] steel

C] aluminium alloy

D] tungsten carbide

69] The least count of a vernier bevel protractor is

A] 1”

B] 5’

C] 1◦

D] 5 ◦

Vernier bevel protractor

70] The part of a vernier bevel protractor which is normally used as a reference base for measuring angles is the

A] Blade

B] Stock

C] Disc

C] Main scale

71] The part of a vernier bevel protector on which main scale divisions are marked is the

A] Stock

B] Dial

C] Disc

D] Adjustable blade

72] The part of a bevel protractor, which comes in contact with the inclined surface while measuring is the

A] Blade

B] Stock

C] Disc

D] Dial

73] The value of each division of the main scale of a vernier bevel protractor is

A] 5’

B] 1◦

C] 5◦

D]10◦

74] The value of each division of the vernier scale of a bevel protractor is

A] 1◦

B] 1◦5’

C] 1◦55’

D] 5’

75] Which of the following is not the part of a combination set?

A] Stock

B] Square head

C] Protractor head

D] Centre head

76] The function of the Pedestal grinder includes ---------

A] Sharpening of the cutting tool

B] Rough grinding

C] Both (a] & (b]

D] None of these

77] The type of abrasives used for the two wheels of Pedestal Grinder are-

A] Coarse and Coarse type

B] Fine and fine type

C] Coarse and fine

D] None of these

78] The Operation of shaping of the grinding wheel by dressers?

A] Dressing

B] Truing

C] Clogging

D] glazing

79] Dressing and truing of the grinding wheel are --------

A] Exactly the same operation
B] Clone with the same equment
C] Done only for coarse grinding wheel
D] Only for form grinding
80] Ribs are given on the unmachined portion of the angle plate for
A] Easy handling
B] Convenience in manufacturing
C] Clamping while setting on machines
D] Rigidity and to prevent distortion
81] The slots on the angle plate are given for
A] Reducing weight
B] Aligning the work
C] Lifting using hooks
D] Accommodating bolts
82] The size of the angle plates is stated by
A] Weight
B] Length
C] Length x width
D] Size number
83] The taper shank drills are held on the machine by means of
A] Chucks
B] Sleeves
C] Drift
D] Vice
84] Drill chucks are fitted on the drilling machine spindle by means of a
A] Knurled ring
B] Arbor
C] Drift
D] Pinion and key
85] The Morse taper provided on drills ranges between
A] MT 1 to MT 5
B] MT 1 to MT 4
C] MT 0 to MT 5
D] MT 0 to MT 4
86] A drift is used for
A] Drawing a drill location
B] Fixing chuck on the machine spindle
C] Removing a broken drill from the work

D] Removing the drill from the machine spindle

87] When the taper shank of the drill is larger than the machine spindle, the device to hold the drill is a

A] Drill sleeve

B] Taper socket

C] Drill drift

D] Chuck and key

88] The suitable cutting fluid for drilling mild steel in a drilling machine is

A] Synthetic soluble oil

B] Neat oil

C] Distilled water

D] Soluble oil

89] A special feature of the radial drilling machine is

A] It can be used for drilling with a HSS drill

B] Table can be moved and set at any position

C] A variety of speeds is available

D] The spindle can be brought to any position

90] The point angle of drills depends on

A] The size of the drill

B] The type of machine

C] The material of the work

D] The RPM of the drill

91] The point angle for a standard drill is

A] 60°

B] 108°

C] 118°

D] 135°

92] The helical angle determines the

A] Cutting angle

B] Chew angle

C] Rake angle

D] Lip angle

93] The clearance angle of the drill is between

A] 3° to 5°

B] 8° to 12°

C] 12° to 20°

D] 15◦ to 20◦

94] In a remote place (no electricity available] a rail track is to be drilled Choose the right drilling machine

A] Radial drilling machine

B] Pillar drilling machine

C] <u>Ratchet drilling machine</u>

D] Sensitive drilling Machine

Drilling

95] A drilling machine used by a carpenter for cabinet making is a

A] Ratchet drilling machine

B] Radial drilling machine

C] <u>Breast drilling machine</u>

D] Sensitive drilling machine

96] Which one of the following drilling machines is used for drilling holes where electricity is not available?

A] Bench drilling machine

B] Pillar drilling machine

C] Redial drilling machine

<u>D] Ratchet drilling machine</u>

97] Which one of the following drilling machine is used for heavy duty work?

A] Bench drilling machine

B] Pillar drilling machine

<u>C] Radial drilling machine</u>

D] Electric hand drilling machine

98] Drill chuck are held on the machine spindle by means of ------

<u>A] arbor</u>

B] Drift

C] draw-in bar

D] Chuck nut

99] Different speeds are obtained in a sensitive bench drilling machine by ----

A] Belt pulley mechanism

B] Hydraulic mechanism

C] Rack and Pinion mechanism

D] Cam and follower mechanism

100] Tap are re sharpened by grinding -----

A] Hutes

B] Threads

C] Diameter

D] Relief

101] The tapping drill size for M10 x 15 is ----------

A] 82

B] 83

C] 84

D] 85

102] A nut is to be made for a screw of M10XIS What should be the size of drilled hole?

A] 8-5 mm

B] 90 mm

C] 95 mm

D] 100 mm

103] A die in which more than one cutting operation is per formed in one stroke

A] Piercing die

B] Progressive die

C] Combination die

D] Compound die

Tap Die

104] A die in which cutting and non cutting operations are carried out per stroke

A] Piercing die

B] Progressive die

C] Combination die

D] Compound die

105] A die in which two or more sequential operations are performed at two or more stations upon the work

A] Piercing die

B] Progressive die

C] Combination die

D] Compound die

106] A die in which the shape of the punch and die are directly reproduced in the metal with little or no metal flow

A] Progressive die

B] Combination die

C] Compound die

D] Forming die

107] The die used for producing any shape of holes

A] Piercing die

B] Progressive die

C] Combination die

D] Compound die

108] A short reamer with an axial hole used with an arbor or mandrel is called -------

A] Parallel reamer

B] Adjustable reamer

C] Expansion reamer

D] Chucking reamer

Reamer

109] Which one of the following machine reamers is used to correct the misalignment between the reamer axis and the work axis?

A] Floating blade reamer

B] Machine jig reamer

C] Shell reamer

D] Chucking reamer

110] The process of enlarging the end of a hole for accommodating the socket screw head is

A] Reaming

B] Spot facing

C] Counter boring

111] Appropriate tool used for spot facing operation is

A] Reamer

B] Counter sinks

C] Fly cutters

D] Lathe tool

112] The cutting speed for aluminium with HSS tools is

A] 30 m/min

B] 50 m/min

C] 70 m/min

D] 130 m/min

113] The cutting speed for brass with a HSS tool is

A] 10 m/min

B] 25 m/min

C] 70 m/min

D] 140 m/min

114] The distance, which the cutting edge of a tool passes over the material in a minute while machining is Know as

A] RPM

B] Feed

C] Machine speed

D] Cutting speed

115] By using coolants on work pieces we can choose

A] Higher cutting speeds

B] lower cutting feeds

C] lower cutting speeds

D] heavy depth of cuts

116] The depth of cut for M24 x 3 mm internal thread is

A] 05412 x 3

B] 06134 x 3

C] 05 x 3

D] 07 x 3

117] The depth of cut for metric square threading is

A] 06 x P

B] 05 x P

C] 05412 x P

D] 06412 x P

Thread

118] To cut buttress thread, the depth of cut is

A] 05412 x P

B] 06 x P

C] 07 x P

D] 075 x P

119] The dial test indicator shows the measurement as

A] The actual size of the component

B] The difference between the two steps of 5 mm

C] The magnified small variations in sizes through a pointer

D] The direct reading of the dimension

120] V -block and dial indicator method is used to measure the

A] Length of the work piece ground

B] Circularity of the surface of the work piece

C] Flatness of the surface

D] Pitch of the thread

121] Which one of the following is not correct about dial test indicator?

A] It has 100 divisions on its dial

B] Motion of the stem is transferred to the dial through Gear train

C] Its accuracy is 01 mm

Dial test indicator

122] Tennon slots are provided on arbor shoulder

A] To facilitate insertion of key between cutter and arbor at any position

‘

B] To facilitate positive power transmission to the arbor

C] To ’ facilitate interchangeability of arbors and machines

D] To avoid loosening of arbor nut during cutting action]

123] In the BIS system of limits and fits, the grade of tolerance are represented by number Symbols and there are ---------i

A] 14 grades of tolerance

B] 16 grades of tolerance

C] 18 grades of tolerance ‘

D] 20 grades of tolerance

Limit fit tolerance

124] A Product is said to have the quality when

A] Its shape and dimensions are within the limit

B] It is fit for use

C] It appears to be very good

D] The choice of material is right

125] The maximum clearance required between hole'30 +0021, 0000 and shaft 30 -0110, 0143 is

A] 0110 mm '

B]0131 mm

C] 0164 mm

D] 0143 mm

126] A dimension is stated as 25 1002 mm in a drawing What is the tolerance?

A] +002 mm'

B] +004 mm

C] -002 mm

D] 2500 mm

127] A pin is fitted in a hole The tolerance zone of the pin is entirely above that of hole The fit obtained will be?

A] Clearance fit

B] Transition fit

C] Interference fit

D] Running fit

128] Tolerance is given to the part size to

A] Production the part within the required permissible size error

B] Increase the production

C] Decrease the Production

D] Finish the components approximately

129] Which one of the following is the clearance fit under the whole basic system?

A] 20 H7/p6‘

B] 2067/211

C] ZOG/gll

D] 20H/g11

130] The three classes of fits as per BIS system aré

A] Clearance fit, interference fit and transition fit

B] Medium fit, push fit and tight fit

C] Flat fit, round fit and square fit

D] ‘Sliding fit ’, loose fit and shrinkage fit

131] Which one of the following tolerance specifications has a maximum dimensionless than 20 mm?

A] 20 +02,-03

B] 20 3202

C] 20 -02, 03 e

D]m 20 +500, ~03

132] Difference between the maximum and minimum limit is --------------------

A] Single informant

B] Basic shaft

C] Clearance

D] Tolerance

133] A shaft 55 running freely in bush bearing the type of fit is ---------

A] Clearance fit

B] Driving plate

C] shrinkage fit

D] None of the above

134] Used for scraping large flat surfaces

A] Bull-nose scraper

B] Three-square

C] Half round scraper

D] None of above

135] Used for scraping small scraper diameter holes and for deburring of holes

A] Bull-nose scraper

B] Three-square

C] Half round scraper

D] None of above

136] Used for scraping bearing surfaces which are neither too big nor too small

A] Bull-nose scraper

B]Three-square

C] Half round scraper

D] None of above

137] Used for scraping large diameter holes

A] Bull-nose scraper

B] Three-square

C] Half round scraper

D] None of above

138] Gun metal is an alloy of copper, ------------

A] tin and zinc

B] Lead and zinc

C] Zinc and nickel

D] Lead and nickel

139] Cast iron is used for manufacturing machine beds because -------

A] it can resist more compressive stress

B] it is heavy in weight

C] It is cheaper metal

D] It is a brittle metal

140] Which one of the following is the resistance of a metal to elastic deformation?

A] Ductility

B] Strength

C] Stiffness

D] Toughness

141] The process of heating and cooling to change the structure of steel for obtaining the required properties is called

A] Hardening

B] Normalizing

C] Heat treatment

D] Tempering

142] The main purpose of annealing is to

A] Increase the hardness

B] Increase the toughness

C] Improve machinability

D] Improve distortion

143] The purpose of normalizing steel is to -----------

A] Remove the induced Stress

B] Improve genes and reduce brittleness

C] Soften the metal

D] Increase the surface?

144] Which one of the following process is used for hardenmg the outer 5" Annealing

A] Hardening

B] Tempering

C] Case Hardening

D] Tear surface

145] The purpose of producmg a component with tough and ductIle core and hard ou is known as

A] Hardening

B] Case hardening

C] Tempering

D] annealing

146] Lower critical temperature of high carbon steel while hardening is ----------

A] 9600C

B] 900°C

c] 7230 c

D] 56O C

147] The process of Changing the structure and thus changing the properties by heating and 'cooling is known as --

A] Heat treatment

B] Alloying

C] Tempering

D] None of these

148] For refining the grain structure which one of the following heat treatment processes 'Is adopted

A] Annealing

B] Hardening

C] Tempering

D] Normalising

149] Annealing is performed on iron and steel ---------

A] To remove internal stresses

B] To reduce hardness

C] To improve machinability

D] All of these

150] Which one of the following does not fall under the stages of heat treatment?

A] Heating

B] Cleaning

C] Quenching

D] Soaking

20] METAL 02

151] Gun metal is an alloy of copper, -----------

A] tin and zinc

B] Lead and zinc

C] Zinc and nickel

D] Lead and nickel

152] for making gutters, roof flashing, hoods etc

A] Galvanised iron

B] Stainless steel

C] Copper sheet

D] Metal sheets

153] in dairies food processing, kitchen ware etc

A] Galvanised iron

B] Stainless steel

C] Copper sheet

D] Metal sheets

154] for making buckets, heating ducts, cabinets etc

A] Galvanised iron

B] Stainless steel

C] Copper sheet

D] Metal sheets

155] in canneries and chemical plants Metal sheets

A] Galvanised iron

B] Stainless steel

C] Copper sheet

D] Metal sheets

156] Alloy steel, good corrosive resistance and welds easily

A] Black iron

B] Galvanised iron

C] Stainless steel

D] Aluminium

157] Cheapest, can be rolled to any desired thickness

A] Black iron

B] Galvanised iron

C] Stainless steel

D] Aluminium

158] Resists against rust bright silvery appearance

A] Black iron

B] Galvanised iron

C] Stainless steel

D] Aluminium

159] Corrodes rapidly Bluish black appearance

A] Black iron

B] Galvanised iron

C] Stainless steel

D] Aluminium

160] For mounting a lathe chuck

A] start it by hand and then turn the power on

B] mount it on by power

C] mount it by hand

D] mount it with the help of a hammer

Lathe chuck

161] How many types of Lathe as per manufacturing?

A] Two

B] Three

C] Four

D] Five

162] How many types of Centre Lathe?

A] Two

B] Three

C] Four

D] Five

163] How many types of production lathe?

A] Two

B] Three

C] Four

D] Five

164] Which type of lathe is Roller Lathe?

A] Bench Lathe

B] Special Lathe

C] Production Lathe

D] Centre Lathe

Lathe machine

165] For mass-production which machine is used?

A] Centre Lathe

B] Production Lathe

C] Special Lathe

D] Engine Lathe

166] Which lathe is used for more accurate job?

A] Centre Lathe

B] Special Lathe

C] Production Lathe

D] Tool Room Lathe

167] The accuracy of Tool Room Lathe is] to Compeer Centre Lathe]

(A] Less

(B] More

(C] Very Less

(D] Equal

168] In Locomotive Assemble Wheel with Axel is turning on Lathe

(A] Centre Lathe

(B] Tool Room Lathe

(C] Wheel Lathe

(D] Gap Bed Lathe

169] Cast iron is used for manufacturing machine beds because -------

A] it can resist more compressive stress

B] it is heavy in weight

C] It is cheaper metal

D] It is a brittle metal

170] Which one of the following operations can't be performed on a Center Lathe?]

A] Turning

B] Thread cutting

C] Gear cutting

D] Taper turning

171] While turning on MS] job which types of good chips produce from cutting tool & material?

A] Spiral chips

B] circular chips

C] long chips

D] straight & long chips

172] Cemented carbide material is...?

A] Ferrous metal

B] non-ferrous metal

C] alloy steel

D] non-ferrous alloy

173] Mandrels are generally used when machining with

A] heavy cuts

B] short facing cuts

C] light cuts

D] boring tools

174] For carbide tip tool turning on hard material it has...ecential?

A] Side Rake angle

B] Zero Rake angle

C] Positive Rake angle

D] Negative Rake angle

175] ....] & ....] Shape job turning in form turning?

A] Plain & V] Shape

B] Squre & Round

C] Concave & Convex

D] V & Round

176] Which part making by form turning of machine?

A] Base

B] Bed

C] Carrage

D] Handles

177] Form turning done for this purpose...?

A] For attractive job

B] for large material cutting

C] for better finishing

D] for smallest cut on job

178] Which type of metal tool use for mass production of form turning?

A] HSS]

B] HCS]

C] Carbide

D] Cementite

179] What is template?

A] One of the cutting operation

B] One of the form turning

C] same figure of the job

D] one of the tool

180] Which purpose use template?

A] For marking & checking

B] for threading

C] for turning

D] for measuring

181] Which material is use for making template?

A] HCS] plate

B] Special tool steel

C] brass or copper

d] GI] sheet or MS] thin sheet

182] ---------------is used for checking shape of component

A] Template

B] Snap gauge

C] Instrument

D] Sine bar

183] Name the tool used to make and finish the leak proof joints of a pipe T joint

A] groover

B] setting hammer

C] creasing hammer

D] round bottom stake

184] Chip breaker in a tool is given

A] 'It break the chips into small pieces

B] to have continuous type of chips from long cut

C] to have crushed chips]

185] Step type chip breaker is the one

A] in which a small groove is ground behind the cutting edge

B] in which a step IS ground on the face of the tool along the cutting edge

C] in which a thin carbide plate or clamp is brazed or screwed on the face of the tool]

186] Sine bar is made of

A] high carbon steel

B] high speed steel

C] nickel steel

D] stabilized chromium steel]

187] Zero Rake angle give for tool?

A] To avoid friction of tool

B] For increase tool life

C] For increase straight of tool

D] For better finishing on job

188] The Gear ratio required for cutting a screw thread of 25 mm on a lathe having a lead screw pitch using single point cutting tool is ----

A] 1:2

B] 2:1

C] 1:1 mm

189] A tumbler gear unit has

A] a single gear

B] two gears

C] three gears

D] four gears

190] Which one is the operation that cannot be done on the slotting machine?

A] key way slotting

B] dovetail slotting

C] gear cutting

D] thread cutting

191] Which one of the feed cannot be given to a slotter table with accessories

A] longitudinal

B] rotary

C] vertical

D] cross

Slotter m/c

192] The size of a slotter is specified by its maximum

A] longitudinal travel of table

B] height between table and ram

C] crosswise travel of table

D] length of stroke of ram

193] To slot a convex surface, the cutting tool required is

A] square nose tool

B] round nose tool

C] keyway tool

D] cornering tool

194] The convex surface can be slotted by using

A] longitudinal feed

B] rotary feed

C] cross feed

D] vertical feed

195] The purpose of quick return mechanism in a slotting machine is to

A] reduce the cutting time

B] have faster return stroke

C] maintain standard cutting speed

D] reduce idle time having faster idle stroke

196] The main feed shaft of a slotting machine is drive by

A] bevel gear mechanism

B] pawl and ratchet wheel mechanism

C] tumbler gear mechanism

D] worm and worm gear mechanism

197] Loaded with spring

A] Plain or box type tool holder

B] Extension tool holder

C] Relieving type tool holder

D] Rotating tool holder]

198] For general purpose work

A] Plain or box type tool holder

B] Extension tool holder

C] Relieving type tool holder

D] Rotating tool holder]

199] Permits indexing for 90° at 4 positions

A] Plain or box type tool holder

B] Extension tool holder

C] Relieving type tool holder

D] Rotating tool holder]

200] For slotting larger circles

A] Plain or box type tool holder

B] Extension tool holder

C] Relieving type tool holder

D] Rotating tool holder]

201] Moves away the tool in the return stroke]

A] Plain or box type tool holder

B] Extension tool holder

C] Relieving type tool holder

D] Rotating tool holder]

202] Drill chuck are held on the machine spindle by means of ------

A] arbor

B] Drift

C] draw-in bar

D] Chuck nut

203] Which one of the following is used to hold the regular Workpice

A] Faceplate

B] Mandrel

c] Three-Jaw chuck

D] Four-Jaw chuck

Lathe chuck

204] The threads on the back side of the four Jaw chuck has type-----of threads

A] Square

3] Trapezoidal

C] V -shape

D] None of these

205] Knurling operation is done at the

A] turning spindle speed

B] high spindle speed

C] 1/3 of the turning spindle speed

D] 1/2 of the turning spindle speed

206] Knurling is the operation of

A] shearing

B] forming

C] turning

D] pressing

207] Taper turning by offsetting the tailstock method can produce

A] an internal taper

B] an internal taper thread

C] an external taper

D] both external and internal tapers

208] By using the taper turning attachment, tapers can be turned with a setting angle up to

A] 10◦

B] 15◦

C] 20◦

D] 30◦

Taper turning attachment

209] The accuracy of a taper is generally checked by means of

A] taper gauges

B] gauge blocks

C] indicator and height gauge

D] 'V' blocks

210] Turning tapers by the compound rest method involves working solely with

Decimal measurements

B fractional measurements

C metric measurements

D angular measurements]

211] Long tapers are produced

A with the taper turning attachment

B with the compound slide

C by setting over the tail stock

D by adjusting the cross slide]

212] The length of turned tapers are checked with

A vernier calliper

B micrometer

C inside callper

D dial test indicator]

213] The disadvantages of taper turning using the com] pound slide are

A] only long tapers can be turned

B] only very large tapers can be turned

C] only manual in feed is possible

D] only short tapers can be turned due to the restrictions of the compound slide]

214] External tapers are checked with

A] limit plug gauge

B] taper ring gauge

C]taper plug gauge

D] thread plug gauge]

taper ring gauge

215] The use of a taper turned on lathe is ----

A] Assist to transmit drive in the assembled parts

B] Used for Assembly and disassembly of parts

C] Give self alignment in the assembled parts

216] Which type of method is used in mass production of production of producing small length of taper?

A] Form tool

B] Compound slide

C] Tailstock offset

D] Taper turning attachment

217] Morse standard taper is one of the internationally accepted standards taper, which is available in numbers from--------

A]1to7

B]1 to 8

C] O to 7

D] 0 to 8

218] Which taper turning method is used for cutting steep taper?

A] Set over method

B] Taper turning attachment

C] Form tool

D] Swivelling the compound rest

219] Morse taper is used in which of the following machine components -

A] Spindles of lathe

B] Spindles of drill machine

C] Shanks of reamers

D] All of these

220] For mass production of the taper which one of the following method is used]

A] Tailstock offset method

B] Taper turning attachment method

C] Form too method

D] Compound slide method

221] The major diameter of the taper is 40 mm, minor diameter is 30 mm] The total length of the job is 100 mm is tapered then offset is given by -

A] 5 mm

B] 75 mm

C] 12 mm

D] 9 mm

Sine bar

222] Sine bar is made of

A] high carbon steel

B] high speed steel

C] nickel steel

D] stabilized chromium steel]

223] Sine bar is used for

A] levelling the job for drilling

B] finding the angle of taper job

C] measuring diameter of holes

D] checking profile of thread]

224] Length of sine bar is the distance between

A] one end to another end of sine bar

B] diagonal cross length of the sine bar

C] centre to centre between rollers

D] outside to outside between rollers]

225] The size of a sine bar is specified by it's

A] weight

B] measurement of width

C] length

D] maximum angle of setting]

226]The purpose of providing a stopper at one end of the sine bar is for

A] easy handling

B] preventing the job from slipping]

C] supporting the slip gauge

D] using as a reference while setting]

227] A sine bar is made with four or five equally'spaced holes on its body] The purpose of these holes is to

A] Handle the sine bar easily

B] Reduce the weight of sin bar

C] Prevent distortion of the top surface of sine bar

D] Give good appearance to the sine bar

228] A sine bar is used for

A] Measuring the diameter of holes '

B] Finding the angle of a taper job

C] Leveling the job for drilling

D] Chuckin'g the profile of a thread

Slip guage

229] For measuring angles using the sine bar the angle framed according to the ratio between the height of slip gauge and the

A] Height of sine bar

B] Number slip gauge

C] Length of sine bar

D] Width of sine bar

230] -----------is used for checking angle within an accuracy of 1]

A] Gauge

B] Sine bar

C] Temple

D] Telescopic gauge

231] Centre line of the contact rollers and datum surface if the sine bar are

A] Same line' '

B] Parallel

C] Inclined

D] Perpendicular

232] The sine bar is made of -

A] High carbon steel

B] Stabilized chromium steel '

C] High speed steel

D] Nicked steel

233] A sine bar with a length of l=200mm is used to check accurately the angle of a Work piece] The angle to be checked: 250 calculate the height 'h' of the slip gauges?

A] 8454mm

B] 8352mm

C] 8181mm

D] 8552mm

234] Which of the following statement is correct?'

A] Gauges are used to check the size

B] Template are used to chuck-the size

C] Gauges are used to measure the size

D] Gauges are used to check shape of component

235] At what standard temperature are the gauges kept in the section?

A] 100 C

B] 20° C

C] 100 F

D] 20° F

236] Which grade of slip gauge is generally used in workshop?

A] Grade 0

B] Grade l

C] Grade H

D] Grade 0

237] As per Indian Standards a special set gauge is used consisting of

A] 81 Pieces

B] 112 Pieces

C] 120 Pieces

D] 130 Pieces

238] The accuracy of reference gauge is

A] 005 mm

B] 001 mm

C] 0001]

D] 00001 mm

239] In case of ant burr on slip gauge, it should be removed by

A] Filling

B] Lapping

C] Scraping

D] Grinding

240] Hardness of slip gauge should be?

A] More than 63 HRC

B] 58 HRC

C] 55 HRC

D] 50 HRC

241]------------- Slip gauge is used for Checking component within an accuracy of 001 mm]

A] Workshop gauge

B] Inspection gauge

C] Reference gauge

D] Ring gauge

242], ------------is used for checking accuracy of precision instrument]

A] Gauge block

B] Fader gauge

C] Sine bar

D] Plug gauge

243] Slip gauge are Cleaned before using to ensure accuracy] What medium will you use for this purpose

A] Oil

B] Thinner

C] Carbon tetrachloride/ White petrol

D] Turpentine oil

244]To check the dimensional accuracy of identical components, a dial test indicator is set-for t 6 Size and used as a comparator] What will you use to set to the dial test indicator?

A] Dial test indicator

B] Teeter gauge

C] Slip gauge

D], surface gauge

245] which one of the following statement about Sine bar is not correct?

A] Uses tow precision rollers kept on either side

B] Made of the Chromium steel

C] The surface is lapped

D] The centrelines of the holes will be inclined to the top surface

246] A slip gauge is a ----------

A] Rectangular block

B] Square block

C] Cubic block

247] In 4th SERIES of slip gauge, which one of the following range is correct in set 46 pieces

A] 10 to 90 mm

B] 1001 101009 mm

C] 101 to 109 mm

D]‘11’to_-19mm

248] In 5th SERIES of slip gauge, which one Of the following range is correct in set 46 pieces –

A] 100to 100 mm ’

B] 1001 to 1009 mm

C] 101 to 009mrn

D] 11 to 9mm

249] In 2NDS SERIES of slip gauge, which one of the following range IS correct in set of 45 pieces-

A] 10 to 90 mm

B] 1001 to 1] 009 mm

C] 101 to 109 mm

D] 11 to 19mm

250] In 3RD SERIES of slip gauge, which one of the following range is correct in set 46 pieces –

A] 100 to 100 mm

B] 1001 to 1009 mm

C] 101 to 109 mm

D] 11 to 19 mm

251] In 1ST SERIES of slip gauge, which one of the following range is correct in set 46 pieces –

A] 0001mm

B] 001mm

C] 01mm

D] 10mm

252] In 2ned SERIES of slip gauge, which one of the following STEP is correct in set of 46 pieces –

A] 0001mm

B] 001 mm

C] 01 mm

D] 1-0 mm

253] In 3rd SERIES of slip gauge, which one of the following STEP Is correct in set 46 pieces

A] 0001mm

B] 001mm

C] 01 mm

D] 10mm

254] Spindle is perpendicular to the work table

A] Horizontal milling machine

B] Vertical milling machine

C] Universal milling machine]

D] Lathe machine

255] The table can be swivelled in horizontal plane

A] Horizontal milling machine

B] Vertical milling machine

C] Universal milling machine]

D] Lathe machine

256] The spindle is horizontal to the work table

A] Horizontal milling machine

B] Vertical milling machine

C] Universal milling machine]

D] Lathe machine

257] Rigid, sturdy and accommodates heavy work

A] Horizontal milling machine

B] Vertical milling machine

C] Universal milling machine]

D] Lathe machine

258] Boring, keyway cutting, profile milling can be done on this machine

A] Horizontal milling machine

B] Vertical milling machine

C] Universal milling machine]

D] Lathe machine

259] Helical grooves and gears can be milled on this machine

A] Horizontal milling machine

B] Vertical milling machine

C] Universal milling machine]

D] Lathe machine

260] Slide movement on the column

A] Longitudinal feed

B] Cross feed

C] Vertical feed

D] Circular feed]

261] Slide movements on the knee

A] Longitudinal feed

B] Cross feed

C] Vertical feed

D] Circular feed]

262] Rotary table

A] Longitudinal feed

B] Cross feed

C] Vertical feed

D] Circular feed]

263] Table traverse]

A] Longitudinal feed

B] Cross feed

C] Vertical feed

D] Circular feed]

264] produces surface perpendicular to the axis of cutter

A] is face milling process

B] is side milling process

C] is plain milling process

D] is end milling process

265] producing surfaces vertical and flat, perpendicular to the machine arbor

A] is face milling process

B] is side milling process

C] is plain milling process

D] is end milling process

266] cutting is done at end and periphery to make slots

A] is face milling process

B] is side milling process

C] is plain milling process

D] is end milling process

267] The process done on plain milling machine

A] is face milling process

B] is side milling process

C] is plain milling process

D] is end milling process

268] The process done on vertical milling machine

A] is face milling process

B] is side milling process

C] is plain milling process

D] is end milling process

269] Composition of cobalt tungsten carbide and tentalum carbide

A] Carbon steel cutters

B] Sintered carbide tool cutters

C] Ceramics cutters

D] Diamond cutters

Milling cutters

270] A composition of oxides of aluminium and silicon or magnesium

A] Carbon steel cutters

B] Sintered carbide tool cutters

C] Ceramics cutters

D] Diamond cutters

271] Steel with11%to 15% carbon

A] Carbon steel cutters

B] Sintered carbide tool cutters

C] Ceramics cutters

D] Diamond cutters

272] Suitable for low cutting speed and feed rates

A] Carbon steel cutters

B] Sintered carbide tool cutters

C] Ceramics cutters

D] Diamond cutters

273] Extremely high cutting speed with low feed rate for precision finishing]

A] Carbon steel cutters

B] Sintered carbide tool cutters
C] Ceramics cutters
D] Diamond cutters
274] More brittle in nature
A] Carbon steel cutters
B] Sintered carbide tool cutters
C] Ceramics cutters
D] Diamond cutters
275] is used to cut flutes on reamers
A] Equal double angle cutter
B] Bore type single angle cutter
C] Unequal double angle cutters
D] shank type single angle cutter]
276] is used to cut dovetail guide ways on a horizontal milling machine
A] Equal double angle cutter
B] Bore type single angle cutter
C] Unequal double angle cutters
D] shank type single angle cutter]
277] is used to cut 'V' grooves
A] Equal double angle cutter
B] Bore type single angle cutter
C] Unequal double angle cutters
D] shank type single angle cutter]
278] has two types as type 'A', type 'B' based on the diameter of the small end
A] Equal double angle cutter
B] Bore type single angle cutter
C] Unequal double angle cutters
D] shank type single angle cutter]
279] is Specified by mentioning two angles
A] Equal double angle cutter
B] Bore type single angle cutter
C] Unequal double angle cutters
D] shank type single angle cutter]
280] may or may not have cutting edges at flat side]
A] Equal double angle cutter
B] Bore type single angle cutter
C] Unequal double angle cutters

D] shank type single angle cutter]

281] Vertical milling attachment

A] <u>face milling, boring, end drilling, 'T' slot milling</u>

B] milling longer milling racks

C] mounted on the face of the column or the over arm

D] vertical milling attachment is provided

Milling attachment

282] For using plain or universal milling machine as a vertical milling machine

A] face milling, boring, end drilling, 'T' slot milling

B] milling longer milling racks

C] mounted on the face of the column or the over arm

D] <u>Vertical milling attachment is provided</u>

283] Vertical attachments enable the horizontal milling machine to perform

A] <u>face milling, boring, end drilling, 'T' slot milling</u>

B] milling longer milling racks

C] mounted on the face of the column or the over arm

D] vertical milling attachment is provided

284] The rack milling attachment and rack indexing attachment used for

A] face milling, boring, end drilling, 'T' slot milling

B] <u>milling longer milling racks</u>

C] mounted on the face of the column or the over arm

D] vertical milling attachment is provided

285] Slotting attachment converts the rotary motion of spindle

A] vertical milling attachment is provided

B] can be turned through 90x in either direction

C] to increase the versatility' of the machine

D] into reciprocating motion

286] Milling attachments are designed]

A] vertical milling attachment is provided

B] can be turned through 90x in either direction

C] to increase the versatility' of the machine

D] into reciprocating motion

287] attachment is useful involving light machining

A] Gear cutting attachment

B] Spherical turning attachment

C] Relieving attachment]

D] None of above

Gear

288] tool advancement is] controlled by the cam profile

A] Gear cutting attachment

B] Spherical turning attachment

C] Relieving attachment]

D] None of above

289] useful for cutting splines etc

A] Gear cutting attachment

B] Spherical turning attachment

C] Relieving attachment]

D] None of above

290] By using coolants on work pieces we can choose

A] higher cutting speeds

B] lower cutting feeds

C] lower cutting speeds

D] heavy depth of cuts

291] Extreme pressure additive (EPA] is mixed with cutting fluid for improving its power of

A] Cooling

B] Lubrication

D] Production of the machined surface

C] Cleaning of cutting zone

292] The main purpose for using a lubricant in machine tools is to ------

A] Cool down the making parts

B] Prevent machine tool from heating

C] Wet the making parts for close contact

D] Minimize the friction between the making parts

293] Preventive maintenance is

A] The maintenance involves the use of sensitive instruments

B] The maintenance generally performed by operator himself

C] The work carried only when machine break down

D] plan to minimize the unforeseen break down

294] What is a break down maintenance?

A] Maintenance to minimize the unforeseen breakdown

B] Maintenance generally performed by operator himself

C] Maintenance involves replacement of worn out parts

D] Repairs work carried only when machine breakdown

295] The Routine Maintenance is ---------

A] it is planned maintenance to minimize the unforeseen breakdown

B] This type of maintenance involves the use of sensitive instrument

C] It is repair work carried only when machine breakdowns

D] This types of maintenance is generally performed by operator himself

296] Lubricant is necessary to

A] run the machine smoothly taking least load

B] Run the machine quickly

C] Stop the machine immediately

D] Produce work piece of greater accuracy

297] The main purpose for using a lubricant in machine tools is to ------

A] Cool down the making parts

B] Prevent machine tool from heating

C] Wet the making parts for close contact

D] Minimize the friction between the making parts

298] Having 5 mm pitch of screw and dividing ratio of 40 : 1 what is lead of milling machine

A] 025 mm

B] 5 mm

C] 8 mm

D] 200 mm

299] The rack milling attachment and rack indexing attachment used for

A] face milling, boring, end drilling, 'T' slot milling

B] milling longer milling racks

C] mounted on the face of the column or the over arm

D] vertical milling attachment is provided

Indexing head

300] Used for rapid method of indexing

A] Direct indexing head

B] Simple indexing head

C] Universal indexing head

D] None of above

301] Used where a large number of identical pieces are indexed

A] Direct indexing head

B] Simple indexing head

C] Universal indexing head

D] None of above

302] Used with a number of change of gears for differential indexing]

A] Direct indexing head

B] Simple indexing head

C] Universal indexing head

D] None of above

303] Grinding wheels made out of---------------- abrasive are most common because of its free and cool cutting action]

A] Aluminium oxide

B] Silicon oxide

C] Ammonium oxide

D] Carbide]

304] Which among the following abrasive is mostly used for cutting off wheels for cutting non metallic materials?

A] Aluminium oxide

B] Silicon carbide

C] Diamond

D] None of above

305] Which abrasive particle is used for

Grinding Wheel

tungsten carbide tool insert?

A] Silicon carbide

B] A|203

C] Diamond

D] Corundum

306] Which of the following is the natural abrasive?

A] Aluminium oxide

B] Silicon

C] Boron carbide

D] Corundum

307] Which of the following is the manufactured abrasive?

A] Corundum]

B] Quartz

C] Silicon

D] Emery

308] Which abrasive particle is used for grinding steel fittings?

A] Silicon carbide

B] Aluminium oxide

C] Diamond]

D] boron oxide

309] What kind of abrasive cut of wheel should be used to cut concrete stone and masonry?

A] Silicon

B] Al203

C] Diamond grit

D] Glass

310] Aluminium oxide wheel is used for grinding ------------

A] cast iron

B] Cemented carbide

C] HSS ‘

D] ceramic

311] The bond of diamond wheel suitable for offhand grinding of the tipped tool is

A] Resinoid

B] Vitrified

C] Shellac

D] Metal

312] Which among the following bonds, is used commonly?

A] Vitrified bond ’

B] Rubber bond

C] Shellac bond

D] Silicate bond

313] The symbol conventionally used for resinoid bond is ~~~~~~~~

A] v

B] R f

C] B

D] E

314] In grinding practice the term "grade of wheel” refers to ---------‘

A] Hardness of the abrasive used

B] Strength of the bond of the wheel

C] Finish 0f the Wheel

D] Hardness of the work pieces

315] Which bond is used in cut of wheels?

A] Rubber

B] Vitrified

C] Resirjoid

D] Shellac

316] Hardness of grinding wheel is determine by ----------

A] the resistance exerted] by the bond against grinding Stress

B] Hardness of abrasive grains

C] Hardness of bond

D] Ability to penetration

317] When it is required to run a Grinding wheel safely at very high speed, which bond should be used? "

A] Vitrified

B] Shellac

C] Silicate

D] resinoid‘ and rubber

318] in surface grinding what is the suitable range of grain size of the grinding wheel for general purpose surface grinding?

A] 20 to 36

B] 46 to 60

C] 80 to 120

D] 150 to 300

319] AS per Indian Standard, the grain '46'comes under the group of «w] -----

A] Coarse

B] Medium

C] Fine

D] Very fine

320] The grit size of the abrasives used in the grinding wheel is usually specified by ----------

A] Hardness number

B] A size of wheel

C] Softness or hardness of the abrasive

D] Mesh number

321] Bench grinder are used for

A] Heavy duty work

B] Heavy and light duty work

C] Light duty work

D] Lather work

322] Bench Grinders are fitted on a

A] Base

B] Table]

C] Wheel guards

D] Conveyor

323] Which one of the following is the most commonly used Precision grinding machines?

A] Surface grinders

B] Tool cutter grinders

C] Cylindrical grinders

D] All of these

324] Surface grinding machine table slides over the ----------

A] 'T' __ 50:

B] 'v' slot

C] 'U' slot

D] Radial slot

325] The purpose of the surface grinder is to

A] Produce curved surface

B] Produce flat surfaces

C] Produce cylindrical surface

D] Produce uneven surface

326] The cylindrical grinding produced may be

A] plain, cylinder and stepped

B] Plan, tapered and cylinder

C] Cylinder, tapered and stepped

327] Which type of grinding wheel is used on tool and cutter grinder to sharpen the milling cutter?

A] Straight cup wheel

B] Flaring cup wheel

C] Dish wheel

D] Saucer wheel

328] is used on tool and cutter Grinders mainly to sharpen milling cutters and reamers

A] Straight cup

B] Haring cup

C] Dish

D] Recessed both sides

329] When using a diamond wheel for cutter grinding, a wheel speed of 1600/mm is recommended] What should be the depth of cut?

A] 0005-0025mm

B] 0025-004mm

C] 004-005mm

D] 005-005mm

330] Which of the following is precision grinding machine?

A] Pedestal grinding machine

C] Cylindrical surface and Tool & Cutter grinding machine

B] Bench grinding machine

D] Hand grinding machine

331] TOOl and cutter are re-shaped by ------------

A] Surface grinding machine

B] tool and cutter grinding machine

C] Cylindrical grinding machine

D] Rotary grinding machine

332] Name the part of a tool and cutter grinder on which wheel head is being mounted]

A] Base

B] Saddle

C] Column

D] Table

333] The error due to faulty centre holes are eliminated by operation of -------

A] Surface grinder

B] centre-less grinder

C] Tool and cutter grinder

D] Cylindrical grinder

334] In centre less grinding, the work piece rest on -----

A] Centre of the chuck

B] Face plate

C] Rest blade

D] Ali of these

335] Which one of the following is not an advantage of centre grinding?

A] Easier handling of the woe piece during loading and unloading

B] Handling of the longer work pieces

C] Both shaft and brittle work piece could be handled

D] Low grinding speed

336] Straight land surface is cut by tool and cutter grinder with-----------------

A] Plain wheel

B] Cup wheel

C] Conical wheel

D] Disc wheel

337] In grinding irregular, curved, tapered, convex and concave surfaces, the grinder used is ~

A] Cylindrical grinder

B] Internal grinder

C] Surface grinder

D] Tool & Cutter grinder]

338] Which type of grinding machine Is used for sharpening of tool is milling cutters/drills/hobs/broaches?

A] Chucking]

B] Tool and cutter

C] Centre less

D] Bench

339] Which type of grinding machine Is used for sharpening of miiling tools?

A] Chucking]

B] Tool and cutter

C] Centre less

D] Bench

340] For re-sharpening of milling cutter in tool and cutter grinder, which one is suitable size grinding wheel?

A] 35 grit size of grinding wheel

B] 46 grit size of grinding wheel

C] 60 grit size of grinding wheel

D] 80 grit size of grinding wheel

341] The pressure of acetylene gas for gas cutting a 10mm MS plate is...

A] 015 kgf/cm2

B] 05 kgf/cm2

C] 10 kgf/cm2

D] 15 kgf/cm2

342] What size of the cutting nozzle you will select for cutting 10mm thick mild steel?

A] 08 mm

B] 12 mm

C] 16 mm

D] 20 mm

343] The angle of filler rod in case of rightward welding technique is...

A] 10 to 20◦

B] 20 to 30◦

C] <u>30 to 40◦</u>

D] 40 to 50◦

344] One of the advantages of the high pressure system of gas welding is...

A] it is cheaper

B] <u>it is portable</u>

C] it is less dangerous

D] it does not require a skilled welder

345] The function of a gas regulator is...

A] get different types of flames

B] mix the gases in the required proportion

C] change the volume of gas flowing to the blow pipe

D] <u>set the working pressure</u>

346] For welding a lap fillet joint in vertical position by gas what should be the angle of below pipe to the line of weld?

A] 30◦ to 40◦

B] 45◦to 50◦

C] 60◦ to 70◦

D] <u>75◦ to 80◦</u>

347] Which metal pipe should NOT be used for passing acetylene gas in order to avoid explosions?

A] galvanized iron

B] stainless steel

C] mild steel

D] <u>cooper</u>

348] he percentage of carbon in acetylene gas is...

A] 99%

B] <u>923%</u>

C] 891%

D] 853%

349] Acetylene gas contains

A] calcium, carbon and hydrogen

B] calcium and hydrogen

C] calcium, carbon, hydrogen and oxygen

D] carbon and hydrogen

250] In an acetylene purifier the sulphureted and phosphorated hydrogen are removed by...

A] pumice

B] water

C] filter wool

D] purifying chemicals

351] One of the functions of flux in gas welding is...

A] dissolve the metal oxides

B] reduce the melting point of mental

C] increase the flame temperature

D] increase the root penetration

352] On which of the following factors, the choice of flux for gas welding depend?

A] type of material to be joined

B] type of edge penetration

C] type of fuel gas

D] type of flame used

353] The divergence allowance required for gas welding a 300mm long copper butt joint is...

A] 1 to 2 mm

B] 2 to 3 mm

C] 3 to 4 mm

D] 4 to 5 mm

354] The type of edge preparation done for gas welding a 4mm thick copper butt joint is...

A] single bevel

B] single V

C] double V

D] square

355] The size of nozzle used to gas weld 315 mm thick aluminium butt joint is...

A] 13

B] 10

C] 7

D] 5

356] What is the value of preheating temperature for gas welding of aluminium?

A] 100 to 120◦C

B] 150 to 180◦C

C] 180 to 200◦C

D] 210 to 250◦C

357] Name the tool used to make and finish the leak proof joints of a pipe T joint

A] groover

B] setting hammer

C] creasing hammer

D] round bottom stake

358] The angle of vee groove of a single vee but joint for cast iron welding is...

A] 60◦

B] 70◦

C] 80◦

D] 90◦

359] Shielded metal arc welding is classified under the process of...

A] electric resistance welding

B] special welding

C] electric arc welding

D] electro gas welding

360] How to specify the size of an electrode holder?

A] by its weight

B] by its shape

C] by its current carrying capacity

D] by the metal used for making it

361] The current set for a 315mm medium coated mild steel electrode is...

A] 50 to 80 amp

B] 90 to 120 amp

C] 120 to 150 amp

D] 150 to 170 amp

362] A long arc is used in...

A] welding with a low hydrogen electrode

B] horizontal position

C] plug or slot welding

D] cast iron welding

363] If the travel speed of electrode is high, which type of weld defect you will get on a T fillet joint?

A] overlap

B] slag inclusion

C] excessive reinforcement

D] lack of root penetration

364] Which weld defect occurs on a lap fillet joint due to improper weaving of the electrode in the covering/final run?

A] crack

B] undercut

C] lack of fusion

D] edge of plate melted off

365] Which one of the following is used in the oxy-arc cutting process?

A] flux coated solid electrode

B] bare wire tubular electrode

C] flux coated tubular electrode

D] bare tungsten arc cutting electrode

366] The electrode holder in a carbon arc cutting equipment is made up of...

A] plain carbon steel

B] galvanized iron

C] aluminium

D] copper

.

INDUSTRIAL TRAINING INSTITUTE

Monthly Test-1, Marks- 20, Date:- ______________

(Every Question Carry Two Marks)

01] In case of bleeding, take treatment Of

A] spray cold water

B] Bandage immediately -----]

C] Enquire about the accident thought treatment

D] cold 3" and rest

02] in case of an accident, the victim should im

A] Asked to take rest

C] Attended immediately

D] leave him

03] First aid is given to an injured or ill person primarily....

A] Save life

B] Prevent further deterioration of the muff's

C] Give best possible comfort

D] All of these

04] Colour code for Bins for waste paper segregation is -----

A] blue Colour

B] Yellow Colour

C] Red Colour

D] Green Colour

05] In Japanese Seiko stands for -------------

A] Shine

B] Sort

C] Standardize

D] Sustain

06] Benefit of SS system is ------

A] Increase in productivity

B] Increase in quality

C] Reduction in wastage of time

D] All of these

07] Safety is ----------

A] nobody's business

B] every bodise business

C] Some bodies business

D] The organization business

08] For basic categories of safety signs are available The meaning of"prohibition" sign ----

A] shows it must not be done

B] Shows what must be done

C] Warns the hazard or danger

D] Gives information of safety provision

09] Which one is a workshop safety?

A] Keep shop floor clean and free from grease, oil or other slippery materials

B] Stop the machine before changing the speed

C] Don't use cracked or chipped tools

D] Don't try to stop a running machine with hand

10] In Personal Protect Equipment (PPE] HELMET is used to

A] protect head

B] Protect eyes

C] Protect hands

D] Protect ears

INDUSTRIAL TRAINING INSTITUTE

Monthly Test-2, Marks- 20, Date:- ______________

(Every Question Carry Two Marks)

1- 17] Which type of fire extinguisher is used to put off general fire?

A] Water type Extinguisher

B] Foam type Extinguisher

C] Dry chemical powder Extinguisher

D] Carbon dioxide (C02] Extinguisher

2-18] One micrometer (U] is equal to...

A] 0.1mm

B] 0.01mm

C] 0.001mm

D] 0.0001mm

3-19] Name the tool used to make and finish the leak proof joints of a pipe T joint

A] groover

B] setting hammer

C] creasing hammer

D] round bottom stake

4-20] Portion of the hammer used for fixing the handle is...

A] Face

B] Peen

C] Cheek

D] Eye hole

5-21] Weight of the hammer for the marking purpose is...

A] 250g

B] 500g

C] 1 kg

D] 2 kgs

6-22] To cut out small apertures which punch and die type of machine is used?

A] shear type nibbler

B] punch type nibbler

C] circular cutting machine

D] guillotine shearing machine

7-23] Scribers are made of...

A] Mild steel

B] High carbon steel

C] Brass

D] Cast iron

8-24] The size of an engineer's vice is specified by the...

A] Length of the movable jaw

B] Width of the jaws

C] Height of the vice

D] Maximum opening of the jaws

9-25] The form of thread used in carpenters vice is...

A] Square

B] Acme thread

C] Sawtooth Thread

D] Knuckle thread

10-26] The convexity of files helps...

A] To file concave surfaces

B] To file convex surfaces

C] To prevent rounding of edges of work

D] The file to become straight when pressure is applied

INDUSTRIAL TRAINING INSTITUTE

Monthly Test-3, Marks- 20, Date:- ______________

(Every Question Carry Two Marks)

1-33] The reason for using cast iron in making 'V' blocks

A] to increase the weight of the block

B] to reduce the cost

C] to reduce the friction

D] to get a good appearance

2-34] For cutting thin tubing, the most suitable pitch of the hacksaw blade is...

A] 1.8mm

B] 1.4mm

C] 1mm

D] 0.8mm

3-35] For cutting solid brass, the most suitable pitch of the hacksaw blade is...

A] 1.8mm

B] 1.4mm

C] 1mm

D] 0.8mm

4-36] A new hacksaw blade after a few strokes becomes loose because of the...

A] Stretching of the blade

B] Wing-nut threads being worn out

C] Wrong pitch of the blade

D] Improper selection of the set of saws.

5-37] While cutting small diameter pipes, it is advisable to watch regularly and ensure that...

A] The cut is along the curved line

B] More saw teeth are in contract

C] The work is not overheated

D] Proper balancing of hacksaw is maintained

6-38] If the drill runs untrue, it will

A] get too hot

B] cut undersize

C] distort the spindle

D] cut an oversized hole

7-39] Running the drill too fast many result in

A] spoiling the cutting edge

B] poor surface finish

C] twisting the tang

D] drilling an oval hole

8-40] A drill with worn land will

A] drill hole oversize

B] drill hole undersize

C] run out of centre

D] drill an accurate hole

9-41] The morse taper provided on drills used on lathe ranges between

A] MT1 to MT5

B] MT1 to MT4

C] MT0 to MT5

D] MT0 to MT4

10-42] Feeding the small drill too fast into the work may result in

A] breaking the drill

B] bending the drill

C] cutting an oval shape hole

D] increased production

INDUSTRIAL TRAINING INSTITUTE

Monthly Test-4, Marks- 20, Date:- ______________

(Every Question Carry Two Marks)

1-50] The point angle of drills depends on...

A] The size of the drill

B] The type of machine

C] The material of the work

D] The RPM of the drill

2-51] The point angle for a standard drill is...

A] 60°

B] 108°

C] 118°

D] 135°

3-52] The helical angle determines the...

A] Cutting angle

B] Chew angle

C] Rake angle

D] Lip angle

4-53] The clearance angle of the drill is between...

A] 3° to 5°

B] 8° to 12°

C] 12° to 20°

D] 15° to 20°

5-54] The relief angle provided behind the cutting edge is called the..

A] Point angle

B] Chisel edge angle

C] Helix angle

D] Clearance angle

6-55] A set of number drill series consists of drills in the following ranges] Indicate the correct range

A] 1 to 40

B] 1 to 50

C] 1 to 80

D] 1 to 100

7-56] In the number drill series, the smallest drill size is...

A] 0.1 mm

B] 0.35 mm

C] 0.5 mm

D] 0.52 mm

8-57] In the number drill series, the largest drill size is...

A] 102 mm

B] 5.791 mm

C] 5.613 mm

D] 5.410 mm

9-58] In the letter drill series, the size of the drill 'A' is equal to ...

A] 13 mm

B] 6.08 mm

C] 6.045 mm

D] 5.944 mm

10-59] In the letter drill series, the largest drill size is equal to...

A] 10.33 mm

B] 10.490 mm

C] 12.01 mm

D] 15.00 mm

INDUSTRIAL TRAINING INSTITUTE

Monthly Test-5, Marks- 20, Date:- _______________

(Every Question Carry Two Marks)

1-66] which one of the following is the most suitable tap for lathe work?

A] spiral tap

B] machine tap

C] hand tap

D] left hand tap

2-67] A die is turned with a

A] die wrench

B] diestock

C] die plate

D] die handle

3-68] A tumbler gear unit has

A] a single gear

B] two gears

C] three gears

D] four gears

4-69] The cutting edge of a solid tool is made of

A] carbon steel

B] mild steel

C] super high speed steel

D] stelite

5-70] The tip of a cemented carbide threading tool is

A] brazed

B] welded

C] soldered

D] clamped to the shank

6-71] Tool will rub against the work surfaces and the cutting force increases when..

A] The clearance angle is more

B] The clearance angel is less

C] The rake angle is more

D] The rake angle is less

7-72] Formation of a chip while cutting is based on the...

A] Rake angle of the tool

B] Clearance angle of the tool

C] Wedge angle of the tool

D] Clearance and wedge angle of the tool

8-73] The suitable cutting fluid for drilling mild steel in a drilling machine is...

A] Synthetic soluble oil

B] Neat oil

C] Distilled water

D] Soluble oil

9-74] Centre drilling is an operation of...

A] Drilling and countersinking

B] Drilling and counter boring

C] Marking the centre location before drilling

D] Enlarging the diameter of a hole

10-75] Shaft ends are centre drilled for...

A] Supporting jobs between centres

B] Lubricating the dead centre

C] Reducing the weight

D] Assisting counter boring

INDUSTRIAL TRAINING INSTITUTE

Monthly Test-6, Marks- 20, Date:- _______________

(Every Question Carry Two Marks)

1-80] The process of enlarging the end of a hole for accommodating the socket screw head is...

A] Reaming

B] Spot facing

C] Counter boring

D] Counter sinking

2-81]While choosing a boring tool for boring a given diameter, select

A] a long tool

B] a short tool

C] a long and stout tool

D] a short and stout tool

3-82] The cutting edge of the boring tool should be set for a small hole so that it is

A] 0.5 mm above the center

B] 0.5 mm below the center

C] 1 mm above the center

D] in the exact center

4-83] Bored holes are to be chamfered by using

A] a drill

B] triangular scraper

C] a cranked boring tool

D] a flat file

5-84] The tool used for boring deep holes is a

A] lathe mandrel

B] sleeve

C] drill

D] auger bit

6-85] The cutting speed for rough boring is the

A] same as rough turning

B] same as drilling

C] same as knurling

D] same as thread cutting

7-86] The reamer is used for...

A] Drilling holes in thin sheets

B] Drilling deep holes

C] Removing burrs

D] Enlarging and finishing holes

8-87] The reamer teeth are unevenly spaced because...

A] They are easy to manufacture

B] They can reduce chattering

C] They help to cut metal gradually

D] They help to remove the reamer easily

9-88] Which among the following is not a capability of reamers?

A] Finishing small holes

B] Finishing any machined profiles

C] Accuracy to closer limits

D] Producing high quality surface finish

10-89] The most important quality of any cutting fluid is

A] emulsification

B] specific heat

C] specific gravity

D] viscosity

INDUSTRIAL TRAINING INSTITUTE

Monthly Test-7, Marks- 20, Date:- ______________

(Every Question Carry Two Marks)

1-95] The depth of cut is given by

A] the top slide

B] the cross-slide

C] the compound slide

D] adjusting the tool

2-96] For mounting a lathe chuck

A] start it by hand and then turn the power on

B] mount it on by power

C] mount it by hand

D] mount it with the help of a hammer

3-97] The morse taper provided on drills used on lathe ranges between

A] MT1 to MT5

B] MT1 to MT4

C] MT0 to MT5

D] MT0 to MT4

4-98] Feeding the small drill too fast into the work may result in

A] breaking the drill

B] bending the drill

C] cutting an oval shape hole

D] increased production

5-99] Number of flutes in a twist drills are --------

A] 1

B] 2

C] 3

D] 4

6-100] Which one of the following drilling machines is used for drilling holes where electricity is not available?

A] Bench drilling machine

B] Pillar drilling machine

C] Redial drilling machine

D] Ratchet drilling machine

7-101] Which one of the following drilling machine is used for heavy duty work?

A] Bench drilling machine

B] Pillar drilling machine

C] Radial drilling machine

D] Electric hand drilling machine

8-102] The suitable cutting fluid for drilling mild steel in a lathe is

A] synthetic soluble oil

B] neat cutting oil

C] distilled water

D] soluble oil+water

9-103] The suitable cutting fluid for precision grinding is

A] Soluble oil

B] Synthetic soluble oil

C] Neat oil

D] Servo Cut's'

10-104] Advantage of using cutting fluid during grinding operation is ------

A] 5000 surface finish

B] Reduction in cutting forces

C] Reduction in hardening of the work piece

D] All of these]

INDUSTRIAL TRAINING INSTITUTE

Monthly Test-8, Marks- 20, Date:- _______________

(Every Question Carry Two Marks)

1-110] Which is correct angle plate used with face plate

(A] Solid Type

(B] Box Type

(C] Adjustable Type

(D] None of them

2-111] Face plate is made from.....]

(A] Mild Steel

(B] Cast Iron

(C] Brass

(D] Aluminium

3-112] Which following accessories is use for odd an uneven job turning?

(A] Three Jaw Chuck

(B] Two Jaw Chuck

(C] Driving Plate

(D] Face Plate

4-113] An irregular shaped work piece is turned on a Lathe] Which one of the following work holding accessories is used?

A] Two Jaw chuck

B] Three Jaw chuck

C] Driving plate

D] Face plate

5-114]The pads of a steady rest are made of

A] carbon steel

B] lead

C] mild steel

D] brass

6-115] A steady rest is used

A] to hold jobs

B] for face plate work

C] to drive the job

D] to support the job

7-116] A follower steady is held on the

A] lathe bed

B] lathe carriage

C] lathe spindle

D] tailstock

8-117] When turning long work pieces, the following is used

A sleeve

B change gear

C steady rest

D bracket]

9-118] Knurling operation is done at the

A] turning spindle speed

B] high spindle speed

C] 1/3 of the turning spindle speed

D] 1⁄2 of the turning spindle speed

10-119] Knurling is the operation of

A] shearing

B] forming

C] turning

D] pressing

INDUSTRIAL TRAINING INSTITUTE

Monthly Test-9, Marks- 20, Date:- ______________

(Every Question Carry Two Marks)

1-125] The number of fundamental deviations in the B.I.S] system are

A] 20

B] 22

C] 25

D] 28

2-126] The number of grade of tolerances in the B.I.S] system are

A] 12

B] 16

C] 18

D] 20

3-127] The size based on which the dimensional deviations are given is called...

A] Actual size

B] Basic size

C] Minimum limit of size

D] Maximum limit of Size

4-128] The size of parts made by .....] for provide interchange ability properties] (A] Measurement System

(B] Trial and Error System

(C] Limit and Tolerance System

(D] None of Them

5-129] Your job taper is correct if it is measured

A above the higher limit

B in between higher and lower limit

C below the lower limit]

6-130] When tolerance given in one side of the basic dimension, it is called --------

A].Tolerance system

B] Unilateral tolerance

C] Bilateral tolerance

D] Allowance System

7-131] A dimension is stated as (025 H7 in a drawing] The lower limit is -----------

A] 24.75 mm

B] 24.85 mm

C] 25.00 mm

D] 25-021 mm

8-132] The measured Size Of the dimensions of a component as called---------

A] Basic size

B] Nominal Size

C] Allowed size

D] Actual size

9-133] In the drawing the dimensions of a shaft is shown 40i 0068/ 0042, which is the size of Shaft within the tolerance?

A] 4.0.64 mm

B] 40.042 mm

C] 40.000 mm

D] 39.998 mm

10-134] In Hole basic system ----------

A] The size of the shaft is made constant

B] The Size of the hole is made constant

C] Only 'allowance is given on the hole

INDUSTRIAL TRAINING INSTITUTE

Monthly Test-10, Marks- 20, Date:- _______________

(Every Question Carry Two Marks)

1-142] A Product is said to have the quality when ....]

A] Its shape and dimensions are within the limit

B] It is fit for use

C] It appears to be very good

D] The choice of material is right

2-143] The maximum clearance required between hole'30 +0.021, 0.000 and shaft 30 -0.110, 0.143 is.

A] 0.110 mm '

B]0.131 mm

C] 0.164 mm

D] 0.143 mm

3-144] A dimension is stated as 25 .1002 mm in a drawing] What is the tolerance?

A] +0.02 mm'

B] +0.04 mm

C] -0.02 mm

D] 25.00 mm

4-145] A pin is fitted in a hole] The tolerance zone of the pin is entirely above that of hole] The fit obtained will be?

A] Clearance fit

B] Transition fit

C] Interference fit

D] Running fit

5-146] Interchange ability is normally applied for? _

A] Repairing of parts

B] Mass production

C] Single piece production

D] All of these

6-147] Tolerance is given to the part size to...........]

A] Production the part within the required permissible size error

B] Increase the production

C] Decrease the Production

D] Finish the components approximately

7-148] Which one of the following is the clearance fit under the whole basic system?

A] 20 H7/p6'

B] 2067/211

C] ZOG/gll]

D] 20H/g11]

8-149] The three classes of fits as per BIS system aré ....] ~]

A] Clearance fit, interference fit and transition fit

B] Medium fit, push fit and tight fit

C] Flat fit, round fit and square fit

D] 'Sliding fit ', loose fit and shrinkage fit

9-150] Which one of the following tolerance specifications has a maximum dimensionless than 20 mm?

A] 20 +0.2,-0.3

B] 20 320.2

C] 20 -0.2, 0.3 e

D]m 20 +500, ~03

10-151] Difference between the maximum and minimum limit is -~-
~~~~-~~~~~ '

A] Single informant

B] Basic shaft

C] Clearance

D] Tolerance

INDUSTRIAL TRAINING INSTITUTE

Monthly Test-11, Marks- 20, Date:- ______________

(Every Question Carry Two Marks)

1-160] The length of turned tapers are checked with

A vernier calliper

B micrometer

C inside callper

D dial test indicator]

2-161] The disadvantages of taper turning using the com] pound slide are

A] only long tapers can be turned

B] only very large tapers can be turned

C] only manual in feed is possible

D] only short tapers can be turned due to the restrictions of the compound slide]

3-162] External tapers are checked with

A] limit plug gauge

B] taper ring gauge

C]taper plug gauge

D] thread plug gauge]

4-163] The use of a taper turned on lathe is ----

A] Assist to transmit drive in the assembled parts

B] Used for Assembly and disassembly of parts

C] Give self alignment in the assembled parts
~~~~

5-164] Which type of method is used in mass production of production of producing small length of taper?

A] Form tool

B] Compound slide

C] Tailstock offset.

D] Taper turning attachment

6-165] Morse standard taper is one of the internationally accepted standards taper, which is available in numbers from--------

A]1to7

B]1 to 8

C] O to 7

D] 0 to 8

7-166] Which taper turning method is used for cutting steep taper?

A] Set over method

B] Taper turning attachment

C] Form tool

D] Swivelling the compound rest

8-167] Morse taper is used in which of the following machine components -...

A] Spindles of lathe

B] Spindles of drill machine

C] Shanks of reamers

D] All of these

9-168] For mass production of the taper which one of the following method is used.......]

A] Tailstock offset method

B] Taper turning attachment method

C] Form too method

D] Compound slide method

10-169] The major diameter of the taper is 40 mm, minor diameter is 30 mm] The total length of the job is 100 mm is tapered then offset is given by -

A] 5 mm

B] 7.5 mm

C] 12 mm

D] 9 mm

INDUSTRIAL TRAINING INSTITUTE

Monthly Test-12, Marks- 20, Date:- ________________

(Every Question Carry Two Marks)

1-190] Which instrument iis used for marking layout?

A] Micrometer

B] Vernier

C] Depth gauge

D] Vernier height gauge

2-191] While marking with a Vernier height gauge, the work piece is generally ----------

A] Supported by an angle plate

B] Supported by another work piece

C] Held by one hand

D] Held without support

3-192] Which of the following is not the part of a combination set?

A] Stock

B] Square head

C] Protractor head

D] Centre head

4-193] A BSW threading tool is to be ground with an included angle of

A] 55◦

B] 60◦

C] 47.5◦

D] 29◦

5-194] The nose radius of a metric 'V' thread tool is

A] 0.144 x P

B] 0.25 x P

C] 0.414 x P

D] 0.0144 x P

6-195] While cutting metric external threads of coarse pitches, it is advisable to swivel the compound rest to

A] 45◦

B] 30◦

C] 60◦

D.90◦

7-196] The depth of B.I.S] metric thread is

A] 0.6403 x P

B] 0.6 x P

C] 0.6134 x P

D] 0.5 x P

8-197] Threading tools are checked for accuracy for the 60◦ angle by using a

A] Thread plug gauge

B] centre gauge

C] screw pitch gauge

D] tool angle gauge

9-198] The number of threads per inch can be checked with a

A] tool gauge

B] metric rule by counting

C] ring gauge

D] screw pitch gauge

10-199] When threading, the carriage is moved along the ways by

A] a gear train on a track

B] the feed rod spline or key-way

C] the lead screw thred

D] the hand wheel

Printed by Libri Plureos GmbH in Hamburg,
Germany